Additional Resources to Accompany
REAL ESSAYS

Eddye S. Gallagher
Tarrant County College

Susan Anker

BEDFORD/ST. MARTIN'S

Boston ♦ New York

Copyright © 2003 by Bedford/St. Martin's

All rights reserved.
Manufactured in the United States of America.

7 6 5 4 3 2
f e d c b a

For information, write: Bedford/St. Martin's
75 Arlington Street, Boston, MA 02116
(617-399-4000)

ISBN: 0-312-40488-3

Contents

Preface for Instructors

Additional Resources to Accompany REAL ESSAYS is designed with your needs in mind. This handy collection of materials for classroom use supplements the materials in *Real Essays* itself.

We have reproduced key pages from *Real Essays* so that you can use them as handouts or make transparencies.

- **Writing Guides,** provided for each of the writing chapters, break down the process for a particular mode into a series of manageable tasks. Each guide includes a series of checklist items that helps students keep track of their progress. (See p. 3.)

- **Quick Review Charts** provide a visual summary of chapter content. (See p. 211.)

We have provided self-assessment tools and diagnostic tests to help you determine where you should focus your instruction.

- **The Writing Questionnaire** gives students the opportunity to reflect on their experience as writers. (See p. 1.)

- **Diagnostic Tests** identify your students' areas of strength and weakness. (See p. 75.)

And we have supplemented the text with tools to provide developmental writers with more step-by-step support, as well as additional grammar exercises and tests for further practice and assessment.

- **Planning Forms for Essays** offer students additional opportunities to visualize and plan their essays. (See p. 45.)

- **Review Tests for Editing Chapters** serve as handy assessment tools, combining all of the strategies covered in each chapter in a single chapter test. (See p. 111.)

- **Supplemental Exercises for Editing Chapters** give you plenty of exercises to supplement each editing chapter. (See p. 159.)

Immediately useful, ultimately practical, *Additional Resources* will help you follow through on the pedagogy of *Real Essays*.

For even more materials, you can visit the companion Web site for *Real Essays,* available at <www.bedfordstmartins.com/realessays>. There you'll find additional resources for developmental professionals, including downloadable forms, outlines, and checklists, as well as information on (and for most, links to) helpful Web sites, list-servs, organizations, and publications. The student portion of the site includes links to Exercise Central—online grammar exercises that provide customized feedback—and the English Research Room, an online resource for research writers.

WRITING QUESTIONNAIRE

Name _____

Course _____ Date _____

Real-World Goals

Use the spaces below to list at least five specific goals you have set for yourself.

_____

_____

_____

_____

_____

_____

_____

Course Goals

Think about your writing and comments you have received about it in the past. What do you think your major problems with writing are? What should you work on improving? List a few answers to these questions in the spaces that follow.

_____

_____

_____

_____

_____

_____

When you have jotted down a few ideas, list three writing skills you want to learn or practice. Be as specific as possible. For example, "Learn to write better" is too general to mean anything much or to help you focus on the areas you want to improve. Based on your answers to the questions above, write three specific skills you want to address and improve during the course.

1. _____

_____

_____

_____

2. _____

_____

_____

_____

3. _____

_____

_____

_____

Writing Guides for Essays
(*Chapters 8–16*)

Chapter 8 Writing Guide: Narration

Follow the steps in this Writing Guide to help you prewrite, draft, revise, and edit your narration. Check off each step as you complete it.

Thinking Critically about Narration

FOCUS Think about who will read your narration and what point you want your readers to understand from your story.

ASK
- What experience or series of events do I want to write about?
- What is important about the story from my point of view?
- What main point do I want to make with this story?
- To make that point, what major events do I need to include?
- What details, examples, and facts will bring these events to life and show my readers what the point is and why it is important?
- Should I include conversation (something that was said)?

Prewrite to Explore your Topic

Prewriting for narration involves considering several possible experiences or stories to retell and deciding on the one that you can bring to life for your readers. Your topic should also reveal something important.

_____ Determine your purpose for writing.

_____ Identify the audience for your essay.

_____ Decide what story you want to tell.

_____ Use a prewriting technique (freewriting, listing/brainstorming, questioning, discussing, clustering) to explore your impressions and thoughts about what happened; how it affected you or others; and what the story shows, explains, or proves.

Write a Thesis Statement

The thesis statement in narration includes the topic and the main point you want to make about it.

Topic	+	Main point	=	Thesis statement
Skydiving		is the most thrilling experience I have ever had.		
The details of my accident		will indicate that the truck driver was at fault.		

_____ Decide what is important, from your point of view, about the story you will tell. Imagine telling your story and hearing someone say, "So what?" How would you respond?

_____ Specify the point you want your readers to understand from your narrative.

_____ Write a working thesis statement that includes your topic and main point.

Support Your Point

Your support in narration includes the major events in your story and the supporting details that explain the events for readers.

_____ List all of the major events in the story.

_____ Review your working thesis statement, and drop any events that do not help you explain, show, or prove your main point. Make your thesis more specific.

_____ Choose at least three major events that will help your readers understand your main point.

_____ Add supporting details about each event that will help your readers experience it as you did. It might help to think about how familiar your readers are with your topic and what details would bring your major events to life for them.

Make a Plan

Making a written plan—an outline—helps you decide how to order your narration. Narration usually tells a story in chronological (time) order, presenting events in the order in which they happened.

_____ Arrange your major events according to when they occurred (in chronological order, first to last).

_____ Write a plan or an outline for your narration that includes your main support points (the major events) and supporting details for each event.

Draft

Drafting a narration means writing in complete sentences and including the following:

- An introduction
- A thesis statement that communicates your topic and main point
- The major events in the story, supported by concrete, specific details

> • A conclusion that reminds your readers of the main point and makes an observation about the importance of the story

_____ Think about how you can show your readers what's important about the story you are telling.

_____ Write an introduction that hooks your readers' interest and presents your thesis statement.

_____ Using your plan or outline, write a topic sentence for each of the main events. Be sure that each topic sentence is directly related to your thesis statement.

_____ Write body paragraphs that include concrete, specific details that further explain your support points and bring the major events of your story to life. Your readers should be able to experience, through the supporting details, the events of the story as you did.

_____ Write a concluding paragraph that reminds your readers of your main point and makes a final observation about the importance of the story.

_____ Title your essay.

Revise

Revising means changing whole sentences or paragraphs to make your writing clearer or stronger. To revise a narration, imagine that you do not know the events in the story or their importance. Read your draft, looking for the following:

- Places where the ideas are off the main point (revising for unity)
- Gaps in information or detail (revising for support and detail)
- Areas in need of "glue" to move readers smoothly from one point to the next (revising for coherence)

_____ Ask another person to read your draft and give you feedback.

_____ Begin revising by considering how you can make the main point of the story clearer or more convincing to your readers.

_____ Reread your thesis statement. Revise to make it clearer, more concrete, and more forceful.

_____ Reread the body of your narration to see if the events and details support your thesis. If you have left out key events that would show, explain, or prove your thesis, add them now. Add any additional supporting details that would help your readers experience the events as you did or as you want them to.

_____ Reread your introduction. Make changes if the opening is dull or lacks force.

_____ Reread your conclusion to make sure that it is energetic and convincing, reminds readers of your main point, and makes an observation on the importance of the story you have told. Your purpose in telling the story should be clear to your readers.

_____ Add transition words and sentences to connect your ideas smoothly.

_____ Make at least five changes to your draft to improve the unity, support, or coherence of your narration or to make the introduction, thesis statement, or conclusion stronger or more convincing.

Edit

Some grammar, spelling, word use, or punctuation errors may confuse your readers and make it difficult for them to understand a point you are trying to make. Even if they do not confuse your readers, errors detract from the effectiveness and overall quality of your writing. Edit your narration carefully, correcting any errors you find.

_____ Ask a classmate or a friend to read your narration and highlight any errors.

_____ Use the spell checker or grammar checker on your computer, but do not rely on those programs to catch all errors.

_____ Read your narration carefully, looking for errors in grammar, spelling, word use, or punctuation. Focus first on sentence fragments, run-on sentences, problems with subject-verb agreement, problems with verbs, and other areas where you know you often make errors.

_____ Print a clean, final copy.

_____ Ask yourself: Is this the best I can do?

Chapter 9 Writing Guide: Illustration

Follow the steps in this Writing Guide to help you prewrite, draft, revise, and edit your illustration. Check off each step as you complete it.

Thinking Critically about Illustration

Focus   Think about what you want to explain and who will read your illustration essay.

Ask
- What main point am I trying to illustrate (explain with examples)?
- Which examples will most clearly and vividly explain my point?
- What examples will my readers most easily understand?
- How can I make the examples specific and detailed?
- How should I order my examples so that they will be the most effective?

Prewrite to Explore Your Topic

Prewriting for illustration involves considering what aspect of a topic you know well enough to illustrate. Then you need to select good examples and make sure that they demonstrate your main point.

_____ Decide on your purpose for writing.

_____ Identify the audience for your essay.

_____ After you select a writing assignment, use a prewriting technique (freewriting, listing/brainstorming, questioning, discussing, clustering) to get some ideas about the topic.

_____ Narrow your ideas to a topic you can write about in a short essay, and then generate examples that would demonstrate your point about the topic.

Write a Thesis Statement

The thesis statement in illustration usually includes the topic and the main point you want to make about it.

Topic	+	Main point	=	Thesis statement
Homeschooling				is beneficial to both the child and the parent.
I would visit Italy,				an enchanting country of diverse landscapes, historic landmarks, and inspiring art master-pieces.

_____ Decide what is important to you about your topic.

_____ Write a working thesis statement that presents your point about what is important.

Support Your Point

The major support points in illustration are the examples you give to demonstrate or prove your thesis. These examples will become the topic sentences for the body paragraphs. To come up with examples, assume someone has read your thesis and asked, "What do you mean?" or "Like what?"

_____ Use a prewriting technique to help you get ideas for examples.

_____ Choose at least three examples that will show your readers what you mean.

_____ Reread your prewriting to find supporting details that you may have already generated.

_____ Find additional supporting details by asking yourself more questions: What do I mean? How? In what ways?

_____ For each of your examples, add supporting details that will help your readers understand how the example demonstrates your main point. Give your readers specific and detailed information about each major example.

Make a Plan

Making a written plan—an outline—helps you decide how to order your illustration. An illustration essay with several examples is often organized by order of importance, building up to the most significant or persuasive example.

_____ Arrange your major support examples in order of importance, leading up to the one that you think will have the most impact on your readers.

_____ Make a plan or outline for your illustration essay that includes your main support points (your examples) and supporting details for each example.

Draft

Drafting in illustration means writing in complete sentences and including the following:

- An introduction with a thesis statement that communicates your topic and your main point about that topic

- The examples that demonstrate or prove your main point
- Supporting details that explain the examples for your reader

_____ Reread your thesis so that it is fresh in your mind.

_____ Write an introductory paragraph that includes your thesis statement and hooks your readers' interest.

_____ Using your plan or outline, write a topic sentence for each of your major examples.

_____ Fill in the supporting details that explain your major support points, your examples. Add any details that occur to you as you write and think about your thesis. Ask yourself what other specific, concrete details would help your readers understand each example as you would like them to.

_____ Write a strong conclusion that refers back to your main point and makes a final observation or recommendation.

_____ Title your essay.

Revise

Revising means changing whole sentences or paragraphs to make your writing clearer or stronger. To revise an illustration, imagine that you are a reader who has no experience with your topic. Read your draft, looking for the following:

- Examples and details that don't really demonstrate your thesis (revise for unity)
- Places where you would stop and think, "I don't get it," because there isn't enough concrete information (revise for support and detail)
- Places where the examples need transitions to connect ideas and move a reader smoothly from one idea to the next (revise for coherence)

_____ Get feedback from others through peer review.

_____ Begin by asking, "If a reader didn't know much about this topic, would my examples give that reader enough information to understand my main point?"

_____ Reread your thesis statement. Revise it so that your point is clearer, more concrete, and more forceful.

_____ Reread the body paragraphs of your illustration essay to see if the examples and supporting details demonstrate your thesis to your readers. Suppose that, after reading your thesis, a reader asked, "How? Give me some examples." Would your body paragraphs supply the answer?

_____ Reread your introduction and make changes if it is dull or weak.

_____ Reread your conclusion to make sure it is energetic and drives home your thesis.

_____ Add transitions, words and sentences that connect your examples and details.

_____ Make at least five changes to your draft to improve its unity, support, or coherence or to make the introduction, thesis statement, or conclusion stronger or more convincing.

Edit

Some grammar, spelling, word use, or punctuation errors may confuse your readers and make it difficult for them to understand a point you are trying to make. Even if they do not confuse your readers, errors detract from the effectiveness and overall quality of your writing. Edit your illustration carefully, and correct any errors you find.

_____ Ask a classmate or friend to read your illustration and highlight errors.

_____ Use the spell checker or grammar checker on your computer, but do not rely on them to catch all errors.

_____ Read your illustration carefully, looking for errors in grammar, spelling, word use, or punctuation. Focus first on sentence fragments, run-on sentences, problems with subject–verb agreement, problems with verbs, and other areas where you know you often make errors.

_____ Print a clean, final copy.

_____ Ask yourself: Is this the best I can do?

Chapter 10 Writing Guide: Description

Follow the steps in this Writing Guide to help you prewrite, draft, revise, and edit your description. Check off each step as you complete it.

Thinking Critically about Description

FOCUS   Think about what you want to describe and the overall impression you want to give your readers.

ASK
- What person, place, or thing do I want to write about? Why? What main impression about my topic do I want to convey?
- Who will be reading this essay, and what do they know or need to know about my topic?
- What thesis statement would introduce my topic and state my main impression?
- To convey my main impression, what aspects of my topic do I need to describe?
- What sensory images will my readers need in order to understand my topic? What details might create those sensory images?

Prewrite to Explore Your Topic

Prewriting for description involves selecting a topic about which you have strong impressions and then getting ideas about those impressions. Description creates strong sensory images in words, allowing your readers to see, feel, or experience your topic as intensely as you have.

_____ Decide on your purpose for writing.

_____ Identify the audience for your essay.

_____ Jot down some ideas about what you see when you visualize your topic.

_____ Think about what main impression you want to convey to your readers.

_____ Use a prewriting technique (freewriting, listing/brainstorming, questioning, discussing, clustering) to explore your impressions and visual or other sensory images.

Write a Thesis Statement

The thesis statement in description includes the topic and the main impression about it that you want to convey to your reader.

Topic	+	Main point	=	Thesis statement
When I take my grandmother's coat from the closet,		it's as if she is standing beside me.		
Overall, the photos		should be colorful, upbeat, and somewhat playful.		

_____ Review your prewriting and decide what main impression you want to create.

_____ Write a working thesis statement that includes your topic and main impression.

Support Your Point

The major support points in description are the sensory images that, together, create the main impression. The sensory images will become the topic sentences for the body paragraphs.

The sensory images are supported by concrete details that allow readers to see, hear, or feel the topic as you do.

_____ Review your thesis statement and prewriting, and make other notes. Try to find strong sensory images that will support your main impression and make the topic come alive for your readers.

_____ Choose at least three sensory images that will help to convey your main impression.

_____ Add specific, concrete details that vividly describe each sensory image. Try to appeal to the senses: sight, sound, smell, touch, taste.

Make a Plan

Making a written plan—an outline—helps you decide how to order your description. A description may use time order, space order, or order of importance, depending on its purpose.

_____ Arrange your support points—your sensory images—in a logical order.

_____ Identify vivid details that will describe each sensory image for your readers.

_____ Make a plan or outline for your description essay.

Draft

Drafting a description means writing in complete sentences and including the following:

- An introduction with a thesis that states your topic and main impression
- Body paragraphs with topic sentences that identify the major sensory images
- Supporting details that show readers each sensory image
- A conclusion that refers back to the main impression and makes a further observation

_____ Close your eyes and try to experience the topic and main impression you are writing about.

_____ Write an introduction that draws your readers in and makes them want to know about your topic.

_____ Write a topic sentence for each of the major sensory images.

_____ Add specific details in each paragraph to bring the sensory images and main impression to life.

_____ Write a conclusion that reminds your readers of your main impression of your topic and makes an observation based on the sensory images you have presented.

_____ Title your essay.

Revise

Revising means changing whole sentences or paragraphs to make your writing clearer or stronger. To revise a description, imagine that you are a reader who has never seen or experienced the topic. Read your draft looking for the following:

- Places where the ideas are off the main point (revise for unity)
- Gaps in information or detail (revise for support and detail)
- Areas in need of transitions to connect ideas and move your readers smoothly from one point to the next (revise for coherence)

_____ Get feedback from others through peer review.

_____ Begin revising by considering how you can make your description more lively or vivid for your readers.

_____ Reread your thesis statement. Revise to convey your main impression more concretely and forcefully.

_____ Reread the body of your essay to see whether the sensory images and details support your thesis. Replace or cut any sensory images that do not support your main impression. Add any supporting details that would help readers understand your main impression of the topic.

———— Reread your introduction. Make changes if the opening is dull or vague.

———— Reread your conclusion to make sure that it is energetic and vivid, reminds readers of your main impression, and makes an observation on the topic you have described. Your purpose in describing the topic should be clear to your readers.

———— Add transition words and sentences to connect your details and lead readers smoothly from one sensory image to another.

———— Make at least five changes to your draft to improve the unity, support, or coherence of your description or to make the introduction, thesis statement, or conclusion stronger or more interesting.

Edit

Some grammar, spelling, word use, or punctuation errors may confuse your readers and make it difficult for them to understand a point you are trying to make. Even if they do not confuse your readers, errors detract from the effectiveness and overall quality of your writing. Edit your description carefully, and correct any errors you find.

———— Ask a classmate or friend to read your description and highlight any errors.

———— Use the spell checker or grammar checker on your computer, but do not rely on those programs to catch all errors. Check spelling and grammar yourself as well.

———— Reread your essay, looking for errors in grammar, spelling, word use, or punctuation. Concentrate especially on finding fragments, run-on sentences, problems with subject–verb agreement, and problems with verb tense.

———— Print a clean, final copy.

———— Ask yourself: Is this the best I can do?

Chapter 11 Writing Guide: Process Analysis

Follow the steps in this Writing Guide to help you prewrite, draft, revise, and edit your process analysis. Check off each step as you complete it.

Thinking Critically about Process Analysis

FOCUS   Think about the process you want to explain to your readers, the steps involved in the process, and the main point you want to make.

ASK
- What process do I know well?
- Who will be reading this, and how much are they likely to know about the process?
- What do I want my readers to be able to do? Should they be able to perform the process themselves? Or should they understand how the process happens?
- Can I write a thesis statement that identifies the process and the main point I want to write about it?
- What steps in the process do my readers need to know about? What details, facts, and examples will help them understand each step?
- How should I arrange the steps?

Prewrite to Explore Your Topic

Prewriting in process analysis involves considering all of the steps involved in doing something or in explaining how something works.

_____ Decide on your purpose for writing.

_____ Identify the audience for your essay. Consider whether your readers will need to follow the steps necessary for the process or want only to understand the process.

_____ Choose a process you understand well. You will need to know all the steps and write about the essential ones in your essay.

_____ Once you know what process you want to explain, use a prewriting technique (freewriting, listing/brainstorming, questioning, discussing, clustering) to jot down some ideas about how to explain that process to a reader who isn't familiar with it.

Write a Thesis Statement

The thesis statement in a process analysis usually identifies the process and the main point you want to make about that process.

Topic	+	Main point	=	Thesis statement
Learning how to use the advanced functions on my computer		is frustrating.		
If you learn how to fall out of love,		you will minimize the pain of a breakup.		

_____ Decide on the main point you want to make about the process. What do you want your readers to know or learn about this process?

_____ Once you know your main point, write a thesis statement that contains both the process(your topic) and your main point about that process.

Support Your Point

The major support points in a process analysis are the essential steps involved in explaining how to do the process or how the process works. These steps should demonstrate the main point about the process that you have stated in your thesis. The supporting details in process analysis explain each of the essential steps to your readers.

_____ List all the essential steps in the process.

_____ Review your thesis statement, and drop any steps that are not essential.

_____ Choose the steps that are necessary for your readers to perform this activity or to understand how it works.

_____ Add details that describe the steps and would help your readers do this activity correctly. Imagine that you are not already familiar with the process, and ask yourself whether you could do it or understand how it works after reading the essay.

Make a Plan

Making a plan—an outline—helps you decide how to order your process analysis. A process analysis generally uses chronological (time) order, presenting each step from first to last as it would take place.

_____ Arrange the steps in the process in chronological order.

_____ Make a plan or an outline for your process analysis essay.

Draft

Drafting in process analysis means writing in complete sentences and including the following:

- An introduction with a thesis statement that identifies the process and the point you want to make about the process
- The essential steps in the process, supported by explanations of those steps
- A conclusion that reminds your readers of your main point and makes another observation about the process

_____ Think about how you can show your readers your main point about the process.

_____ Write an introductory paragraph that includes your thesis statement and hooks your readers' interest.

_____ Write a topic sentence for each of the steps.

_____ Write body paragraphs that explain each step in detail to your readers.

_____ Write a concluding paragraph that has energy, refers back to your point about the process, and makes a final observation or recommendation.

_____ Title your essay.

Revise

Revising means changing whole sentences or paragraphs to make your writing clearer or stronger. To revise a process analysis, imagine that you have no idea how to perform the process or how the process works. Read your draft, looking for the following:

- Places where the essay strays from the essential steps and details about those steps (revise for unity)
- Places where readers might not understand the steps (revise for support and detail)
- Places where transitions are needed to help readers move smoothly from one step to the next (revise for coherence)

_____ Get feedback from others through peer review.

_____ Begin revising by asking yourself how you could make the steps of the process clearer for your readers.

_____ Reread your thesis statement to see whether it clearly identifies the process and your main point about it.

_____ Reread the body of your essay to make sure you haven't left out any essential steps. Add any details that would make the steps clearer.

_____ Reread your introduction, and make changes if it is dull.

    _____ Reread your conclusion to be certain that it is energetic and re-inforces your opening and your thesis.

    _____ Add your transition words and sentences to connect your steps and lead readers smoothly from one to another.

    _____ Make at least five changes to your draft to improve the unity, support, or coherence of your process analysis or to make the introduction, thesis statement, or conclusion stronger or more convincing.

Edit

Some grammar, spelling, word use, or punctuation errors may confuse your readers and make it difficult for them to understand a point you are trying to make. Even if they do not confuse your readers, errors detract from the effectiveness and overall quality of your writing. Edit your process analysis carefully, and correct any errors you find.

    _____ Ask a classmate or friend to read your process analysis and highlight any errors.

    _____ Use the spell checker or grammar checker on your computer.

    _____ Look yourself for additional errors in grammar, spelling, word use, or punctuation. Focus first on sentence fragments, run-on sentences, problems with subject–verb agreement, problems with verbs, and other areas where you know you often make errors.

    _____ Print a clean, final copy.

    _____ Ask yourself: Is this the best I can do?

Chapter 12 Writing Guide: Classification

Follow the steps in this Writing Guide to help you prewrite, draft, revise, and edit your classification essay. Check off each step as you complete it.

Thinking Critically about Classification

FOCUS   Think about what you want to classify (sort) for your readers and the main point you want to make about that topic.

ASK
- Who will be reading this piece of writing, and what do they know or need to know about my topic?
- What is my purpose—my reason for sorting or classifying? What is my main point about the topic?
- To accomplish my purpose, how should I sort things? What should my organizing principle be?
- What categories will help my readers make sense of my topic?
- What people or items fit into each category? What examples, facts, and details will my readers need to understand how I have classified things?

Prewrite to Explore Your Topic

Prewriting in classification involves considering how to sort your topic into useful categories and thinking about how to give good examples of or details about those categories.

_____ Decide on your purpose for writing.

_____ Identify the audience for your essay.

_____ Select the topic or group that you want to classify

_____ Once you have decided on a narrowed topic, use a prewriting technique (freewriting, listing/brainstorming, questioning, discussing, clustering) to generate useful categories for sorting your topic. In classification, a variation on the technique of clustering is often useful: filling in a diagram like the one shown here.

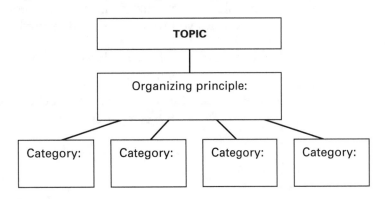

Write a Thesis Statement

The thesis statement in a classification essay can take one of several forms:

Topic   +   Organizing principle = Thesis statement

At most video stores, the videos are arranged by type of film.

Some Japanese researchers claim that people's personalities can be classified by their blood types.

Topic + Organizing principle + Categories = Thesis statement

At most video stores, the videos are arranged by type of film such as comedy, drama, and horror.

Topic   +   Categories   =   Thesis statement

At most video stores, the videos are arranged into categories such as comedy, drama, and horror.

_____ Decide what you want to accomplish by sorting your topic into categories.

_____ Write a thesis statement that follows one of the suggested formats above.

Support Your Point

The support points in classification are the categories into which you choose to sort your topic. These will become the topic sentences for the body paragraphs in your essay. The supporting details will be specific examples of people or items that fit into the categories. Use the diagram below to fill in categories you want to use and examples of each category.

_____ Choose at least three useful categories into which you can sort your topic.

_____ Add facts and details for each example you want to use under the categories.

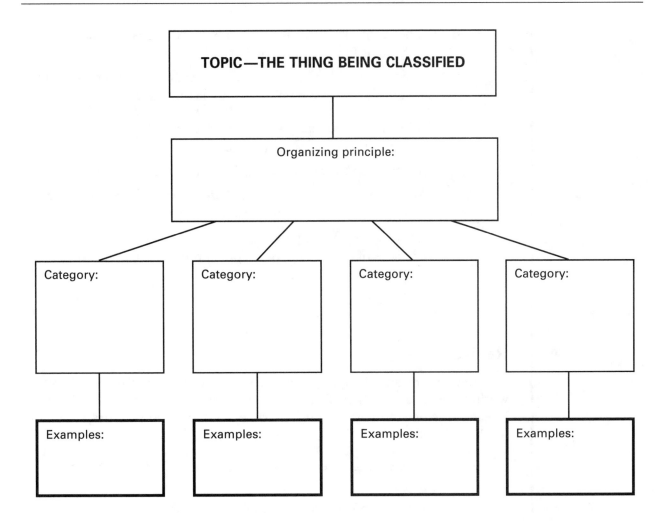

Make a Plan

Making a written plan—an outline—helps you decide how to order your classification. If you have filled in the diagram, you already have a written plan. Now you need to decide on a logical sequence of categories that accomplishes your purpose and will make sense to your readers. (Writers of classification essays may or may not use standard organizational patterns such as chronological order, spatial order, and order of importance.)

_____ Arrange the categories in a logical order.

_____ Make a new diagram that shows the order you have chosen.

Draft

In classification, drafting involves writing in complete sentences and including the following:

- An introduction with your thesis statement

- The categories you have chosen with examples and details of items that fit into those categories
- A conclusion that reminds your readers of your main point and makes an observation about your classification

_____ Write an introductory paragraph that includes your thesis statement and hooks your readers' interest.

_____ Write a topic sentence for each of the categories.

_____ Write body paragraphs that include topic sentences and specific examples and details about each category.

_____ Write a concluding paragraph that reminds your readers of the purpose of classifying your topic into these categories and makes a further observation.

_____ Title your essay.

Revise

Revising means changing whole sentences or paragraphs to make your writing clearer or stronger. To revise a classification essay, imagine that you have no idea how or why one might sort your topic. Read your draft, looking for the following:

- Places where the ideas are off the main point (revising for unity)
- Gaps in information or detail (revising for support)
- Areas in need of transitions that will help readers move smoothly from one point to the next (revising for coherence)

_____ Get feedback from others through peer review.

_____ Begin revising by considering how to make your classification clearer or more interesting for your readers.

_____ Reread your thesis statement. See whether it is clear about what the single organizing principle is, the categories into which you will sort your topic, or both.

_____ Reread the body paragraphs of your classification essay. Replace or cut any categories that do not follow your organizing principle.

_____ Look at the examples you have used in each category. Add details or replace examples to make sure that they will help your readers understand the kinds of things that fit into the category.

_____ Reread your introduction, and make changes if it is dull. Even when you're just introducing categories, be enthusiastic about what you're classifying.

_____ Reread your conclusion with the same goal: to make it energetic and memorable to your readers. Make your final observation a personal comment about the classification system.

_____ Add transitions and transitional sentences to help your readers move smoothly from one category to another.

_____ Make at least five changes to your draft to improve the unity, support, and coherence of your classification or to strengthen your introduction, thesis statement, or conclusion.

Edit

Some grammar, spelling, word use, or punctuation errors may confuse your readers and make it difficult for them to understand a point you are trying to make. Even if they do not confuse your readers, errors detract from the effectiveness and overall quality of your writing. Edit your classification carefully, and correct any errors you find.

_____ Ask a classmate or friend to read your classification and highlight any errors.

_____ Use the spell checker and grammar checker on your computer, but do not rely on those programs to catch all the errors.

_____ Look yourself for errors that the spell checker or grammar checker didn't catch. Focus first on sentence fragments, run-on sentences, problems with subject–verb agreement, problems with verbs, and other areas where you know you often make errors.

_____ Print a clean, final copy.

_____ Ask yourself: Is this the best I can do?

Chapter 13 Writing Guide: Definition

Follow the steps in this Writing Guide to help you prewrite, draft, revise, and edit your definition. Check off each step as you complete it.

Thinking Critically about Definition

FOCUS   Think about what the term you are defining means to you and what it is likely to mean to your readers.

ASK
- Who am I writing this for, and how familiar are my readers likely to be with the term I'm defining?
- What is my purpose in defining this term? Do I want to give a formal definition, or do I want to explain what I mean when I use the word?
- What basic definition should I use?
- What examples or other information about the term will make the meaning clear to my readers?

Prewrite to Explore Your Topic

Prewriting for definition involves coming up with various meanings of the term or concept you are going to define. Most words have more than one meaning, and you want to decide how you want to present your topic.

_____ Decide on your purpose for writing.

_____ Identify the audience for your essay.

_____ Look up the dictionary meaning of the word you might define.

_____ Use a prewriting technique (freewriting, listing/brainstorming, questioning, discussing, clustering) to come up with the different uses of the word. Decide on the meaning you will develop in your essay.

Write a Thesis Statement

The thesis statement in a definition essay often follows one of three basic patterns. You do not have to follow these patterns exactly, but they provide a simple guide to what a thesis statement in a definition essay might include.

1. **Term** + *means/is* + **Basic definition** = Thesis statement

Marriage is the legal union of two individuals.

Customer-oriented means that from start to finish to follow-up, the customer comes first.

2. **Term + Class + Detail = Thesis statement**

Marriage is an institution that legally unites two individuals.

3. **Term + *is not* + Expected definition = Thesis statement**

Marriage is not a life of carefree romance and candlelit dinners.

This last pattern is a little tricky, but if used correctly, it can grab your readers' attention.

_____ Review your ideas about the term, and decide what basic definition you will give or whether you want to give several different meanings.

_____ Do not just copy the dictionary definition. Write the definition in your own words, and think about what wording will make sense to your readers.

_____ Write a thesis statement that includes both the term and your basic definition.

Support Your Point

The major support points in definition are the examples that show what you mean by your use of the term or concept you are defining. The supporting details are the explanations and specific details that you give about each of your examples. These examples and explanations show your readers what you mean by the term. Think about what kinds of examples will make sense to them.

_____ Use a prewriting technique to find examples and details that explain what you mean by the term.

_____ Choose at least three good examples that demonstrate your use of the term being defined.

_____ Explain each example with details that clearly show how the example demonstrates your definition.

Make a Plan

Making a written plan—an outline—helps you decide how to order your definition. A definition generally uses order of importance, arranging the examples to build up to the one with the most impact on readers.

_____ Arrange your examples (your support points) according to which you think best demonstrates the meaning of your term.

_____ Make a plan or outline for your definition essay.

Draft

Drafting a definition means writing in complete sentences and including the following:

- An introduction with a thesis statement
- Examples of the term with specific details that demonstrate your definition of the term
- A conclusion that reminds your readers about your definition

_____ Write an introductory paragraph that includes your thesis statement and gets your readers' interest.

_____ Write a topic sentence for each of the examples.

_____ Write body paragraphs with topic sentences and specific, concrete details about each example.

_____ Write a concluding paragraph that reminds your readers of the term and its meaning and that makes a final observation.

_____ Title your essay.

Revise

Revising means changing whole sentences or paragraphs to make your writing clearer or stronger. To revise a definition, remember that most words can mean different things, depending on how they are being used. Remind yourself of other possible meanings so that you can make sure that your examples clearly explain your particular definition. Read your draft, looking for the following:

- Places where the ideas are off the main point (revising for unity)
- Gaps in information or detail (revising for support and detail)
- Areas in need of transitions to help the reader move smoothly from one point to the next (revising for coherence)

_____ Get feedback from others through peer review.

_____ Begin revising by considering how you can make your definition clearer and more precise for your readers.

_____ Reread your thesis statement. Revise it so that both the term and your definition are clear.

_____ Reread the body of your essay to make sure the examples support your definition and the details about the examples demonstrate what you mean. Add other examples and details that would help explain what you mean by the term.

_____ Reread your introduction to make sure that it has energy and uses concrete words to define your topic.

_____ Reread your conclusion, again judging its energy and interest level. Make a further comment or observation about the topic or definition.

_____ Add transitions and transitional sentences to connect your examples.

_____ Make at least five changes to your draft to improve the unity, support, or coherence of your definition, or to make the introduction, thesis statement, or conclusion clearer or more interesting.

Edit

Some grammar, spelling, word use, or punctuation errors may confuse your readers and make it difficult for them to understand a point you are trying to make. Even if they do not confuse your readers, errors detract from the effectiveness and overall quality of your writing. Edit your definition carefully, and correct any errors you find.

_____ Ask a classmate or friend to read your definition essay and highlight any errors.

_____ Use the spell checker and grammar checker on your computer.

_____ Look yourself for errors that the spell checker or grammar checker didn't catch. Focus first on sentence fragments, run-on sentences, problems with subject–verb agreement, problems with verbs, and other areas where you know you often make errors.

_____ Print a clean, final copy.

_____ Ask yourself: Is this the best I can do?

Chapter 14 Writing Guide: Comparison and Contrast

Follow the steps in this Writing Guide to help you prewrite, draft, revise, and edit your comparison and contrast. Check off each step as you complete it.

Thinking Critically about Comparison and Contrast

FOCUS   Think about what you want to compare or contrast and the main point you want to make about your subjects.

ASK
- What are my readers likely to know about these subjects?
- What do I want my readers to be able to do: make a decision or understand my subjects?
- What are some parallel points of comparison or contrast between my two subjects? Which points will best help me to achieve my purpose?
- Which of the two organizations would best help me get my point across: point-by-point or whole-to-whole?

Prewrite to Explore Your Subjects

Prewriting for comparison and contrast involves considering what subjects to compare or contrast and then coming up with some points of comparison or contrast for them.

_____ Decide on your purpose for writing.

_____ Identify the audience for your essay.

_____ Select two subjects with similarities and differences you want to explore.

_____ Decide whether you want readers to choose between or to understand your two subjects.

_____ Consider whether the subjects have enough in common to allow a valid comparison or contrast between them.

_____ Once you decide what subjects to compare or contrast, use a prewriting technique (freewriting, listing/brainstorming, questioning, discussing, clustering) to explore in what ways the subjects are alike or different.

Write a Thesis Statement

The thesis statement in a comparison/contrast essay includes the two subjects you are comparing or contrasting and the main point you want to make about them.

Subject /Subject   +   Main point   =   Thesis statement

The ages of twenty and forty are both enjoyable, but they represent very different stages in life.

The job offers I received from Company A and Company B are both good, but they differ on a number of points.

_____ Decide why you are comparing and contrasting the subjects and what's important about the comparison and contrast.

_____ Write a thesis statement that includes your subjects and the main point you want to make about them.

Support Your Point

The major support points in comparison and contrast are the points of comparison that you use. The supporting details are the specific details and explanations you give about the points of comparison or contrast.

_____ Review your ideas about the subjects.

_____ List some differences or similarities, depending on whether you are comparing, contrasting, or doing both.

_____ Select from your list the points of comparison that you will use in the essay, choosing points that your readers will understand and that serve your purpose. These points of comparison are the major support points for your thesis statement.

_____ Add supporting details and examples to explain the points of comparison.

Make a Plan

Making a written plan—an outline—helps you decide how to order your comparison and contrast. A plan for a comparison/contrast essay must use either point-by-point organization or whole-to-whole organization. Your plan should follow one of the structures shown here:

POINT-BY-POINT	WHOLE-TO-WHOLE
Thesis statement	Thesis statement
Topic sentence, point 1	Topic sentence, subject 1
subject 1	point 1
subject 2	point 2
Topic sentence, point 2	point 3
subject 1	Topic sentence, subject 2
subject 2	point 1
Topic sentence, point 3	point 2
subject 1	point 3
subject 2	Concluding statement
Concluding statement	

_____ Decide whether you will use a point-by-point or whole-to-whole organization.

_____ Make a plan or outline that follows the point-by-point or whole-to-whole structure as shown here.

Draft

Drafting a comparison/contrast essay means writing in complete sentences and including the following:

- An introductory paragraph that includes your thesis statement about your two subjects
- Body paragraphs that explain your points of comparison
- A concluding paragraph that reinforces your thesis

_____ Think about what is interesting about the comparison you are about to make.

_____ Write an introductory paragraph that introduces your two subjects and the main point you will make about them. Try to spark your readers' attention.

_____ Write a topic sentence for each of the points of comparison or contrast.

_____ Write body paragraphs that provide specific details about the points of comparison so that your readers can understand the similarities or differences between your two subjects.

_____ Write a concluding paragraph that refers back to your main point and makes a further comment or observation based on your points of comparison or contrast.

_____ Title your essay.

Revise

Revising means changing whole sentences or paragraphs to make your writing clearer or stronger. To revise your comparison/contrast essay, imagine that you know little about the subjects. Read your draft from that perspective, looking for ways to make the similarities or differences clearer. Read your draft, looking for the following:

- Places where the ideas are off the main point (revising for unity)
- Gaps in information or detail (revising for support and detail)
- Areas in need of transitions to help readers move smoothly from one point to the next (revising for coherence)

_____ Get feedback from others through peer review.

_____ Reread your thesis. Make sure it presents the two subjects forcefully and clearly, and states the point you want to make in your essay.

_____ Reread the body paragraphs. Add other points of comparison and contrast or details that would clearly demonstrate your main point. Add details that would show the similarities or differences between the subjects.

_____ Make sure that you have followed either point-by-point or whole-to-whole organization all the way through your essay.

_____ Reread your introduction. If it lacks energy or clarity, rewrite it to give it some life.

_____ Reread your conclusion to make sure that it sounds energetic, confirms your main point about the two subjects, and makes a further observation.

_____ Add transitions that move your readers from one point of comparison to another, and decide whether you want to repeat key words.

_____ Make at least five changes to your draft to improve the unity, support, or coherence of your comparison and contrast or to make the introduction, thesis statement, or conclusion stronger or more convincing.

Edit

Some grammar, spelling, word use, or punctuation errors may confuse your readers and make it difficult for them to understand a point you are trying to make. Even if they do not confuse your readers, errors detract from the effectiveness and overall quality of your writing. Edit your comparison and contrast carefully, and correct any errors you find.

_____ Ask a classmate or friend to read your essay and highlight any errors.

_____ Use the spell checker and grammar checker on your computer.

_____ Look yourself for errors that the spell checker or grammar checker didn't catch. Focus first on sentence fragments, run-on sentences, problems with subject–verb agreement, problems with verbs, and other areas where you know you often make errors.

_____ Print a clean, final copy.

_____ Ask yourself: Is this the best I can do?

Chapter 15 Writing Guide: Cause and Effect

Follow the steps in this Writing Guide to help you prewrite, draft, revise, and edit your cause and effect essay. Check off each step as you complete it.

Thinking Critically about Cause and Effect

FOCUS   Think about a topic that matters to you and whether you want to describe its causes, its effects, or both.

ASK
- Who are my readers? Who are the people that I am writing for?
- Are my causes *real* causes, not just events that happened before? Are my effects *real* effects, not just events that follow?
- What examples and details do I need to give in order to make the causes and effects stand out?
- How should I organize the essay? Should I arrange the causes and effects by order of importance, chronologically, or in some other way?

Prewrite to Explore Your Topic

Prewriting for cause and effect involves thinking about the actual causes of an event or the actual results of it, as opposed to an event that came before another event but didn't really cause it or came after it but was not an effect of it.

_____ Decide on your purpose for writing.

_____ Identify the audience for your essay.

_____ Jot down some ideas about a situation that affects you. Using the ring diagram as a prewriting technique works well for cause and effect.

_____ Consider how the situation occurred and what will happen because of it.

Write a Thesis Statement

The thesis statement in a cause/effect essay usually includes the topic and your main point about it. To state your main point clearly in a cause/effect essay, you might use a word such as *because, cause, reason, result,* or *effect* in your thesis statement.

Topic   +   Main point   =   Thesis statement

Irresponsible behavior caused my car accident.

Note that the writer groups the items in the "causes" ring in the ring diagram for this topic into the more general term *irresponsible behavior.*

The health of one of my patients, George Hanson, is being seriously affected by conditions in the offices of Kirkland Brothers.

_____ Determine whether you are writing about causes, effects, or both.

_____ Decide what point you want to convey about the situation's causes or effects.

_____ Write a thesis statement that presents the situation or event and the main point you want to make about the causes or effects.

Support Your Point

The major support points in a cause/effect essay are the causes, effects, or both that you present to demonstrate your main point.

The supporting details explain how the cause or effect you have identified directly caused the situation or resulted from it. The explanations are important because they tell your readers *how* the causes or effects relate to the situation.

_____ List the most important causes or effects of a situation.

_____ For each cause or effect, give an example and details about how it caused or resulted from the event or situation. Think about what information and explanation your reader needs to know.

Make a Plan

Making a written plan—an outline—helps you decide how to order your cause and effect. A cause/effect essay often uses order of importance to arrange causes or effects. By building up to the most important point, the essay creates a strong final impression on readers.

_____ Make a plan or outline for your essay that arranges the causes and effects in order of importance, from least to most significant, or in some other logical order.

_____ Include explanations of each cause and effect in your plan.

Draft

Drafting a cause/effect essay means writing in complete sentences and including the following:

- An introduction with a thesis statement that communicates your topic and main point about it
- The causes, effects, or both for the situation with detailed explanations
- A conclusion

_____ Think about how you can present the causes or effects so that your readers clearly understand your main point.

_____ Write an introductory paragraph that includes your thesis statement and interests your readers in finding out more about the causes or effects of a particular situation or event.

_____ Write a topic sentence for each of the causes or effects.

_____ Write body paragraphs that present and carefully explain each cause or effect.

_____ Write a strong conclusion that refers back to your main point and makes a final observation.

_____ Title your essay.

Revise

Revising means changing whole sentences or paragraphs to make your writing clearer or stronger. To revise a cause and effect essay, imagine that you have no idea what caused or resulted from the situation. Read your draft looking for the following:

- Places where the ideas are off the main point (revising for unity)
- Gaps in information or detail (revising for support and detail)
- Areas in need of transitions to move readers smoothly from one point to the next (revising for coherence)

_____ Get feedback from others through peer review.

_____ Begin revising by asking yourself how you could make your causes and effects clearer for your readers.

_____ Reread your thesis statement, and make changes so that it has more impact on your readers.

_____ Reread the body of your cause/effect essay to see whether the causes or effects are directly related to the situation or event. Be sure that each is clearly explained, based on what you know about your readers. Add other details that would help explain the causes or effects.

_____ Reread your introduction to make sure that it is as effective as possible.

_____ Reread your conclusion to make sure that it is energetic and convincing, that it reminds your readers of your main point, and that it makes a final observation.

_____ Add transition words and sentences to connect your ideas and lead readers smoothly from one to another.

_____ Decide whether repeating key words would increase your emphasis.

_____ Make at least five changes to your draft to improve the unity, support, or coherence of your cause/effect essay or to make the introduction, thesis statement, or conclusion stronger or more convincing.

Edit

Some grammar, spelling, word use, or punctuation errors may confuse your readers and make it difficult for them to understand a point you are trying to make. Even if they do not confuse your readers, errors detract from the effectiveness and overall quality of your writing. Edit your cause/effect essay carefully, and correct any errors you find.

_____ Ask a classmate or friend to read your cause/effect essay and highlight any errors.

_____ Use the spell checker and grammar checker on your computer.

_____ Look yourself for errors that the spell checker or grammar checker didn't catch. Focus first on sentence fragments, run-on sentences, problems with subject–verb agreement, problems with verbs, and other areas where you know you often make errors.

_____ Print a clean, final copy.

_____ Ask yourself: Is this the best I can do?

Chapter 16 Writing Guide: Argument

Follow the steps in this Writing Guide to help you prewrite, draft, revise, and edit your argument. Check off each step as you complete it.

Thinking Critically about Argument

FOCUS   Before and as you write, think about your position on the issue and how you can persuade your readers.

ASK
- Who will be reading this essay, and what are they likely to know about the issue?
- Why is this issue important to me? What do I have at stake?
- What is my position on the issue?
- What are my reasons for taking this position?
- What are some reasons for the opposing position?
- What is my readers' position?
- How can I build and maintain enthusiasm for my position?
- What facts, statistics, examples, and expert opinions can I include to convince readers of my position?

Prewrite to Explore Your Issue

Prewriting for argument involves exploring an issue you care about and deciding what your position on that issue is. As you prewrite, also think about the reasons you hold a particular view.

_____ Decide on your purpose for writing.

_____ Identify the audience for your argument.

_____ Jot down some ideas about an issue that is important to you, focusing on what your position is and why. Various prewriting techniques work well for argument, so you should choose the one that you are most comfortable with. Freewriting, listing/ brainstorming, and clustering work well for many writers.

_____ Take a few minutes to build some energy about the issue. How does this issue affect you personally? Why does it matter to you?

Write a Thesis Statement

The thesis statement of an argument essay usually includes the issue and the writer's position on that issue. Writers may also use a thesis statement to preview the reasons they will offer to support their position.

Issue   +   Position   =   Thesis statement

The minimum wage should be raised.

Issue	+	Position	+	Reasons	=	Thesis statement

The minimum wage should be raised because it is too low for workers to afford the basic necessities.

As you develop and revise your argument, you will also need to revise your thesis statement, right up to the very end, making it clearer and more forceful each time.

Support Your Point

The major support points in an argument are the reasons you give for your position on the issue. These reasons will become the topic sentences for the body paragraphs of your essay. The supporting details in argument are the evidence and information you provide for each of your reasons. To come up with convincing support, keep a specific audience in mind, particularly readers who may not care about the issue or (if they do care) may not share your position on the issue.

_____ Use a prewriting technique to come up with support (convincing reasons and evidence) for your position. Look for persuasive facts, statistics, examples, and expert opinions to support your position.

_____ Clearly state each reason and give specific evidence and details to back it up.

_____ Acknowledge the opposing position and show weaknesses in it by addressing points an opponent might raise.

_____ Consider whether you will need to use outside sources.

_____ Test your reasons and evidence.

_____ Reread your reasons and evidence from your opponents' point of view, looking for weaknesses in your argument. Anticipate your opponents' objections, and include evidence to answer those objections.

_____ Consider every important angle of the issue.

_____ Make sure that your reasons support your position and that your evidence supports your reasons.

Make a Plan

Making a written plan—or outline—helps you decide how to order your argument. The reasons in an argument essay are generally arranged by order of importance. As you organize, think about what your audience will find most convincing. Be sure to acknowledge and address opposing positions, too.

_____ Arrange your reasons according to their importance to your position. End with the most important reason.

_____ Make a plan or outline with your reasons and evidence in order.

Draft

Drafting an argument essay means writing in complete sentences and including the following:

- An introduction, including a thesis statement that presents your position on an issue
- Major reasons for your position
- Evidence and information that support your reasons
- An acknowledgment of the opposing view with responses to it
- A conclusion

_____ Think about how your readers might react to each point you make.

_____ Write an introductory paragraph that includes your thesis statement and interests your readers in the issue.

_____ Using your outline or plan, write a topic sentence for each of the reasons that will support your position on the issue.

_____ Write body paragraphs that give facts, examples, and expert opinions that support your reasons.

_____ End on a strong note. Before writing your conclusion, build up your energy and enthusiasm again (see p. 244). Save your best reason for last, and write a conclusion that refers back to your issue and position, reviews the support you give, and makes a final strong statement urging your readers to see it your way and act accordingly.

_____ Title your essay.

Revise

Revising means changing whole sentences or paragraphs to make your writing clearer or stronger. To revise an argument, assume that you are someone who holds the opposing view but is willing to listen to the other side. Think about how to make your reasons and evidence more convincing to that kind of a reader. Read your draft, looking for the following:

- Places where the ideas are off the main point (revise for unity)
- Gaps in information or detail (revise for support and detail)

- Areas in need of transitions to help the reader move smoothly from one reason to the next (revise for coherence)

_____ Get feedback from others through peer review. Ask one or more readers to listen carefully to your reasons and to challenge any that they find weak or don't understand. Find new reasons and evidence if needed.

_____ Begin revising by asking yourself how you could make your argument clearer and more persuasive for your readers.

_____ Reread your thesis to make sure that you clearly state your position on the issue.

_____ Reread your topic sentences to make sure that they clearly support your position and are written in strong, concrete language. Focus on whether you could provide additional reasons that would convincingly support your position.

_____ Reread each body paragraph to see if the evidence you give clearly explains and backs up your reasons. Add other evidence and information that might further persuade your readers that your reasons are valid.

_____ Reread your introduction to make sure that it states a definite opinion, with confidence, and hooks your readers' interest.

_____ Reread your conclusion to make sure that it sounds energetic and convincing, reminds your readers of your position, and makes a final attempt to persuade your readers.

_____ Add transitions to help your readers move smoothly from one reason to the next and to connect the backup evidence you provide.

_____ Decide whether repeating key words would increase your emphasis.

_____ Make at least five changes to your draft to improve the unity, support, or coherence of your argument or to make the introduction, thesis statement, or conclusion stronger or more convincing.

Edit

Some grammar, spelling, word use, or punctuation errors may confuse your readers and make it difficult for them to understand a point you are trying to make. Even if they do not confuse your readers, errors detract from the effectiveness and overall quality of your writing. Edit your argument carefully, and correct any errors you find.

_____ Ask a classmate or friend to read your argument and highlight any errors.

_____ Use the spell checker and grammar checker on your computer.

_____ Look yourself for errors that the spell checker or grammar checker didn't catch. Focus first on sentence fragments, run-on sentences, problems with subject–verb agreement, problems with verbs, and other areas where you know you often make errors.

_____ Print a clean, final copy.

_____ Ask yourself: Is this the best I can do?

Planning Forms for Essays
(*Chapters 8–16, 21*)

Prewriting on Your Purpose and Audience

Prewrite to find answers to these questions before you write any paper. Prewrite again later if it seems helpful. Keep your responses in mind as you draft and revise your paper.

PURPOSE

- What is my assignment? What topic will I be writing about?

- What point do I want to make about my topic?

- What do I want my audience to think about my topic?

- What do I need to tell my audience so that they will get my point?

AUDIENCE

- Who is my audience?

- What does my audience already know about my topic?

- What does my audience want or need to know about my topic?

- Does my audience have a particular attitude or opinion about my topic? Do I need to address that specifically?

Clustering Form

Use this form when you are clustering to explore a topic. Write your narrowed topic in the center circle. Then write three ideas or questions about that topic in the three circles that connect to the center circle. Add three more ideas about each of those items in the circles that connect to them, and so on.

You can add more circles and lines as you need them. In the beginning, try to add at least three items at each level. As you progress in your clustering, you may want to focus on a certain part of your cluster.

For more about using clustering to explore ideas, see Chapter 2 in *Real Essays.*

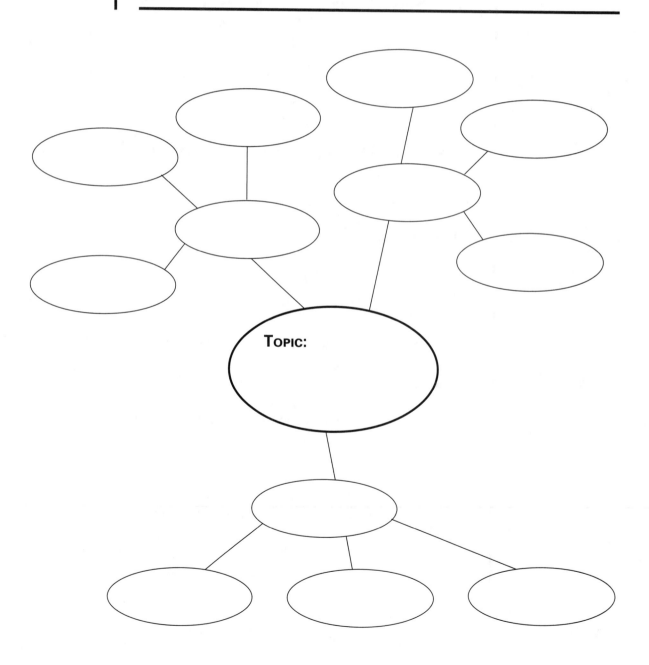

TOPIC:

Essay Outline

   I. Introduction

      A. Thesis: _____

      B. Method of getting reader's attention: _____

  II. Topic sentence for first support paragraph: _____

    _____

      A. Supporting idea 1: _____

      B. Supporting idea 2: _____

      C. Supporting idea 3: _____

 III. Topic sentence for second support paragraph: _____

    _____

      A. Supporting idea 1: _____

      B. Supporting idea 2: _____

      C. Supporting idea 3: _____

 IV. Topic sentence for third support paragraph: _____

    _____

      A. Supporting idea 1: _____

      B. Supporting idea 2: _____

      C. Supporting idea 3: _____

  V. Conclusion

      A. Main point: _____

    _____

      B. Method of linking back to introduction: _____

    _____

Planning Form for Narration

Narration is writing that tells a story of an event or experience that has some importance.

The **thesis statement** for narration usually includes the topic and a preview of what is important about it. The **support** for narration is a series of events. Use details to show readers your point of view about why this story is important.

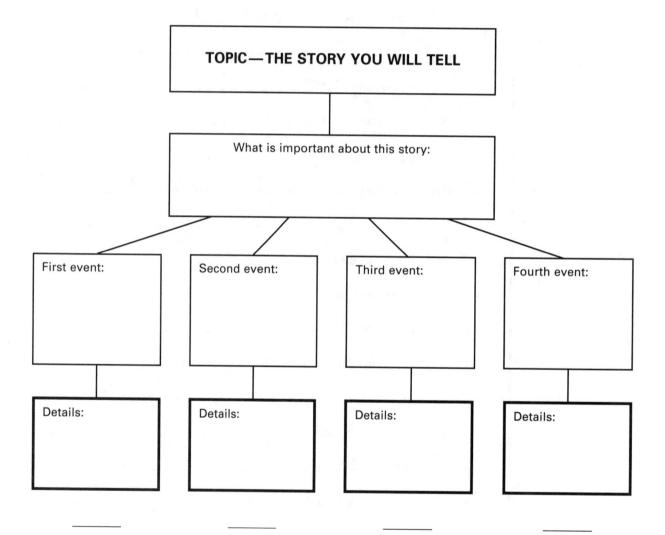

Narration usually uses **chronological (time) order.** If the order of the events in your paper will be different from the order in which you wrote them down here, use the lines under the boxes to write in numbers indicating the order you want to use.

For more help with your narration paper, see Chapter 8 in *Real Essays.*

Planning Form for Illustration

Illustration is writing that uses examples to show, explain, or prove a point.

The **thesis statement** for illustration usually includes the topic and the point the writer wants to make about it.

The **support** for illustration is a series of examples or a single example explained thoroughly. Use details to bring your examples to life.

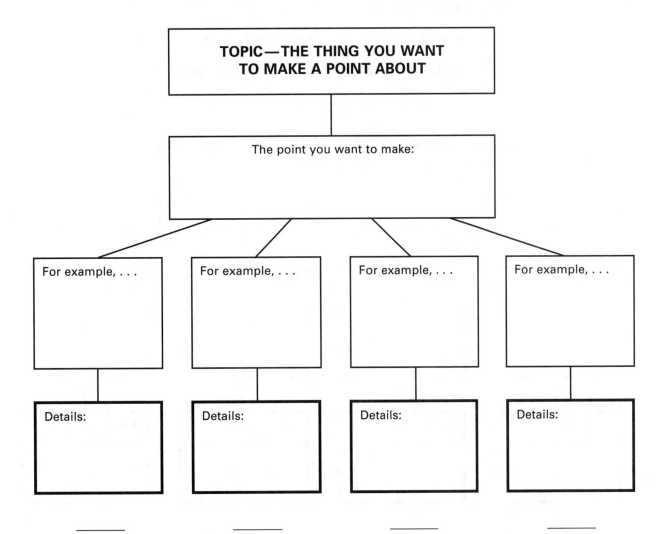

Illustration can use **chronological order (time order), spatial order (space order),** or **order of importance.** If the order of the examples in your paper will be different from the order in which you wrote them down here, use the lines under the boxes to write in numbers indicating the order you want to use.

For more help with your illustration paper, see Chapter 9 in *Real Essays*.

Planning Form for Description

Description is writing that creates a clear and vivid impression of the topic.

The **thesis statement** for description usually includes the topic and conveys the main impression about it that you want to communicate to your readers. The **support** for description is the sensory details that contribute to the main impression. Use additional information to make the details more concrete and specific.

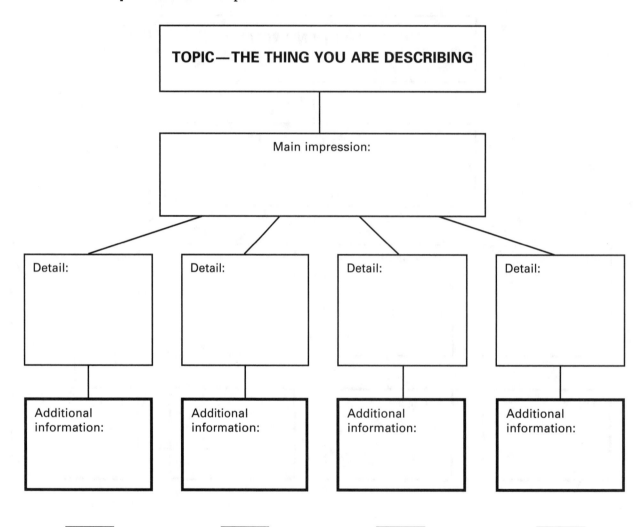

Description can use **chronological (time) order, spatial (space) order,** or **order of importance.** If the order of the details in your paper will be different from the order in which you wrote them down here, use the lines under the boxes to write in numbers indicating the order you want to use.

For more help with your description paper, see Chapter 10 in *Real Essays*.

Planning Form for Process Analysis

Process analysis is writing that either explains how to do something or explains how something works.

The **thesis statement** for process analysis usually includes the process and the point you want to make about it. The **support** for process analysis is a series of steps. Use details to make the steps easier to imagine and follow.

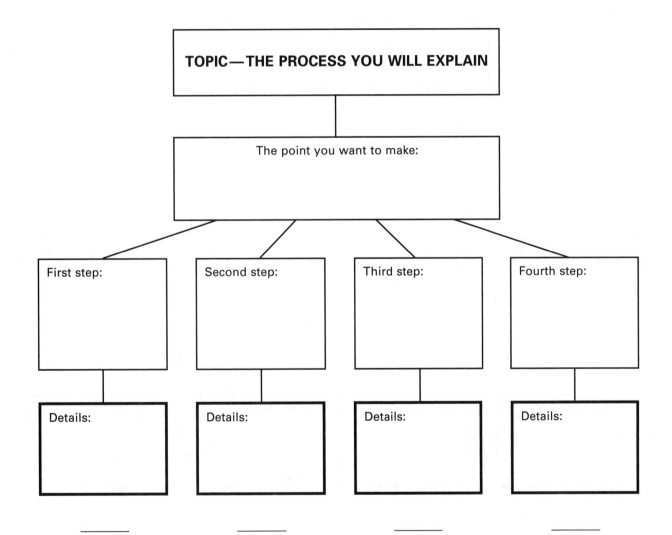

Process analysis usually uses **chronological (time) order.** If the order of the steps in your paper will be different from the order in which you wrote them down here, use the lines under the boxes to write in numbers indicating the order you want to use.

For more help with your process analysis paper, see Chapter 11 in *Real Essays.*

Planning Form for Classification

> **Classification** is writing that organizes, or sorts, things into categories. The **thesis statement** for classification usually includes the topic being classified and the organizing principle used to organize it. Sometimes the categories themselves are named. The **support** for classification is a group of categories that all follow a single organizing principle. Use examples to show what you mean by each category.

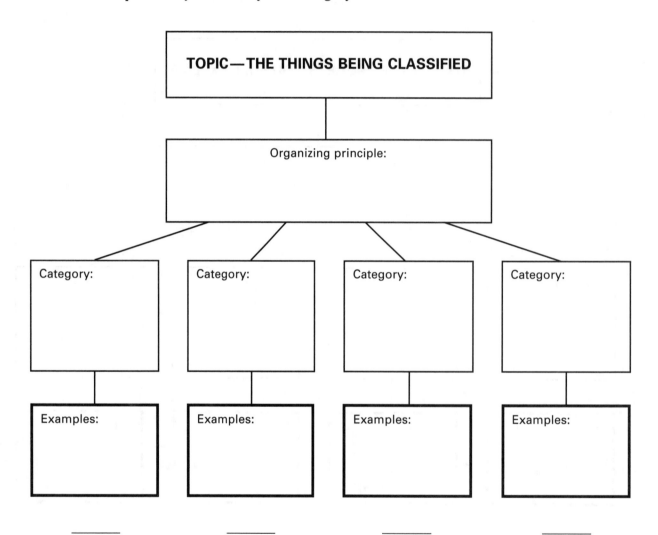

> Classification can use **chronological (time) order, spatial (space) order,** or **order of importance.** If the order of the categories in your paper will be different from the order in which you wrote them down here, use the lines under the boxes to write in numbers indicating the order you want to use.
>
> For more help with your classification paper, see Chapter 12 in *Real Essays*.

Planning Form for Definition

Definition is writing that explains what a term means.

The **thesis statement** for definition usually includes the term and a brief, basic definition. The **support** for definition is details and examples that help readers see what you mean.

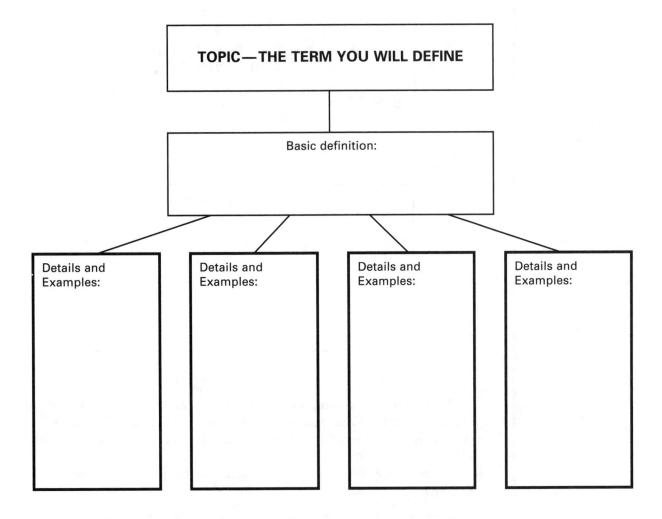

TOPIC—THE TERM YOU WILL DEFINE

Basic definition:

Details and Examples:

Details and Examples:

Details and Examples:

Details and Examples:

Definition generally uses **order of importance.** If the order of the examples in your paper will be different from the order in which you wrote them down here, use the lines under the boxes to write in numbers indicating the order you want to use.

For more help with your definition paper, see Chapter 13 in *Real Essays*.

Planning Form for Comparison and Contrast

Comparison is writing that shows the similarities among things; **contrast** shows the differences.

The **thesis statement** for comparison/contrast usually identifies the subjects and tells the main point you want to make about them.

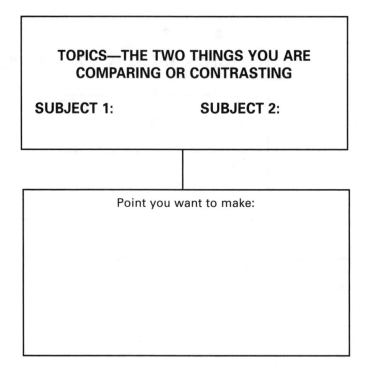

TOPICS—THE TWO THINGS YOU ARE
COMPARING OR CONTRASTING

SUBJECT 1:   SUBJECT 2:

Point you want to make:

The **support** in a comparison/contrast is a series of important, parallel points of similarity or differences between the two subjects. Comparison/contrast usually uses one of two standard **organizations:** point-by-point or whole-to-whole.

For more help with your comparison/contrast paper, see Chapter 14 in *Real Essays.*

Point-by-Point Organization for Comparison and Contrast

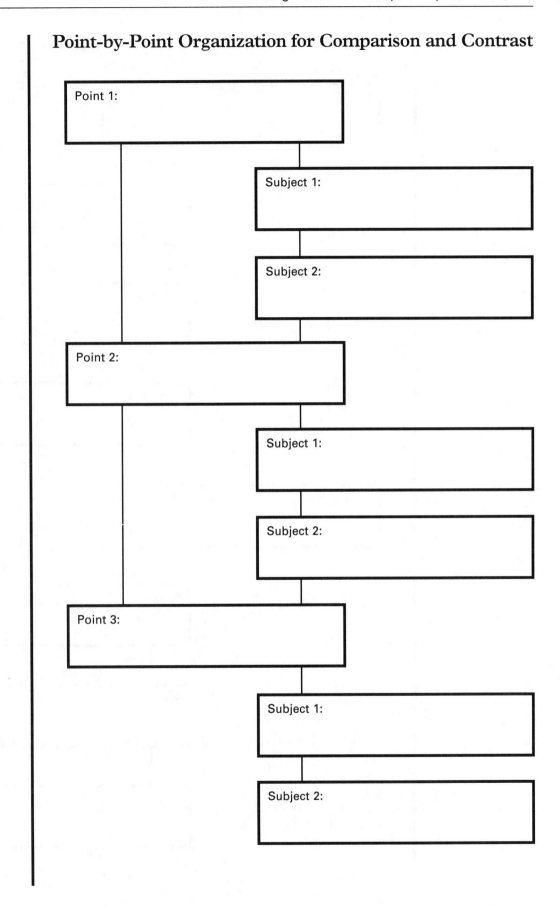

Point 1:

Subject 1:

Subject 2:

Point 2:

Subject 1:

Subject 2:

Point 3:

Subject 1:

Subject 2:

Whole-to-Whole Organization for Comparison and Contrast

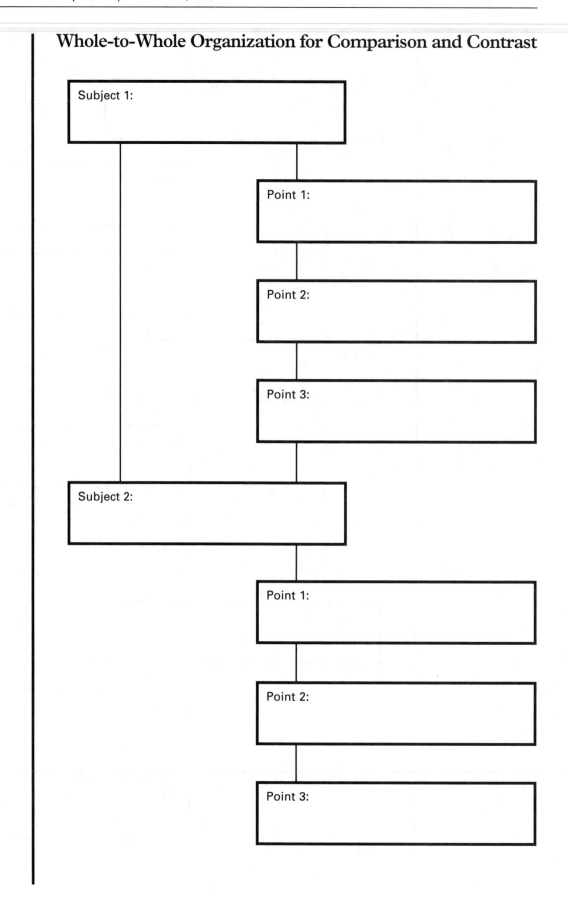

Planning Form for Cause and Effect

Cause/effect is writing that explains what made an event happen (cause) and/or what happened as a result of the event (effect).

The **thesis statement** for cause/effect should include the event or situation and indicate whether you will discuss the causes, the effects, or both. The **support** for cause/effect will include major causes and/or effects of the situation or event. The writer must make sure that there is a true cause/effect relationship, not just something that happened before or after another event. For a stronger paper, choose details and examples that are significant.

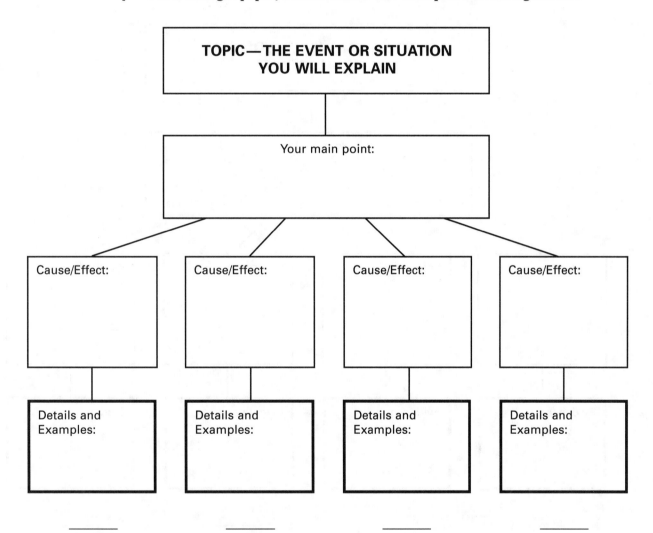

TOPIC—THE EVENT OR SITUATION
YOU WILL EXPLAIN

Your main point:

| Cause/Effect: | Cause/Effect: | Cause/Effect: | Cause/Effect: |

| Details and Examples: | Details and Examples: | Details and Examples: | Details and Examples: |

Cause/effect writing is often organized by **order of importance.** If the order of the causes/effects in your paper will be different from the order in which you wrote them down here, use the lines under the boxes to write in numbers indicating the order you want to use.

For more help with your cause/effect paper, see Chapter 15 in *Real Essays.*

Planning Form for Argument

Argument is writing that takes a position on an issue and defends it with evidence to persuade someone else of the position.

The **thesis statement** for argument should include the issue and your position on that issue. The **support** for argument is reasons and evidence that persuade readers that your position is a good one. Use details and examples to make your evidence concrete and persuasive.

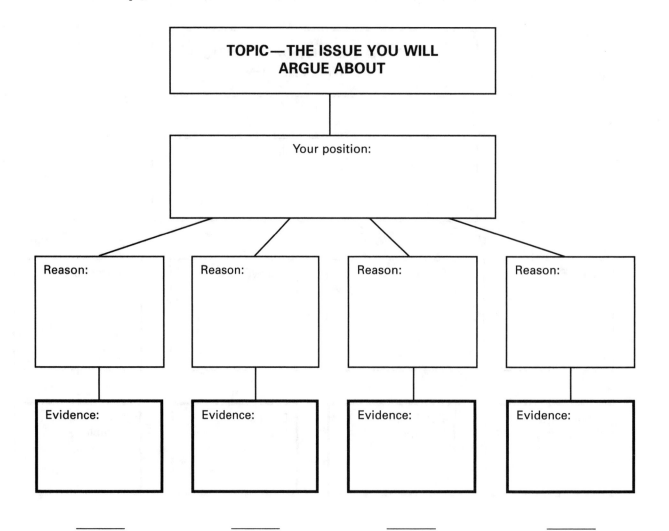

Argument usually uses **order of importance.** If the order of the pieces of evidence in your paper will be different from the order in which you wrote them down here, use the lines under the boxes to write in numbers indicating the order you want to use.

For more help with your argument paper, see Chapter 16 in *Real Essays.*

Planning Form for Research Essay

Research is finding information that will help you or others understand a subject.

The **thesis statement** for a research essay should include the narrowed topic and the point you want to make about it. The **support** for a research essay will include evidence you gather through personal research (e.g., interviews, personal knowledge) and secondary research (e.g., materials from the library or the Internet). For a more persuasive paper, choose details and examples that are significant.

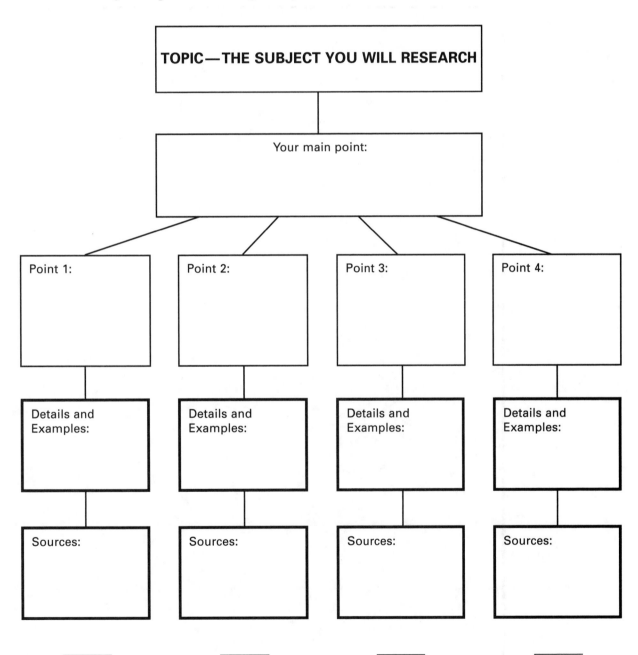

TOPIC—THE SUBJECT YOU WILL RESEARCH

Your main point:

Point 1:	Point 2:	Point 3:	Point 4:
Details and Examples:	Details and Examples:	Details and Examples:	Details and Examples:
Sources:	Sources:	Sources:	Sources:

Because topics and purposes are so varied when conducting research, the resulting essay could follow almost any of the writing strategies (e.g., illustration, comparison/contrast, cause/effect, argument, definition) that you have studied so far. Therefore, a research essay can be organized in a number of ways, depending on the purpose of the research. The most common forms would include **chronological (time) order, spatial (space) order,** or **order of importance.** If the order of the major points in your paper will be different from the order in which you wrote them down here, use the lines under the boxes to write in numbers indicating the order you want to use.

For more help with your research essay, see Chapter 21 in *Real Essays*.

Peer Review Evaluation Form

TO BE COMPLETED BY STUDENT WRITER:

Your name:

Title of the paper:

One or two focused questions for the reviewer (optional):

TO BE COMPLETED BY THE STUDENT REVIEWER:

Your name:

1. What is the writer's main point?

2. What is the strongest part of the paper? Why is it good?

3. What could be improved? How could it be better?

4. Were any parts confusing?

5. Did you want to learn more about anything?

6. What are your responses to any questions the writer asked you above?

7. Do you have any other comments?

Supplemental Exercises for Chapter 20 (*"Finding, Evaluating, and Documenting Sources"*)

20-1: Integrating and Citing Sources within Your Paper

When using information you have gathered from other sources, you may want to use direct quotes, indirect quotes, summaries, or paraphrases. You also need to make sure that you do not plagiarize (use the author's exact words without using quotation marks and/or referencing the source). Using the following passage, write on separate paper or your computer a one-sentence summary of the entire passage, a paraphrase of the part of the passage that is in bold type, and a direct quote that could be used in a research essay about the effects of music on the brain. (Be sure to introduce the quote with a signal phrase.) At the end of your summary, paraphrase, or quote, include a parenthetical reference to the original source.

ORIGINAL SOURCE

Music has charms to soothe a savage breast, but scientists are finding that it works those charms through the brain. At a recent conference of the New York Academy of Sciences, [Sandra] Trehub and dozens of other scientists interspersed their PET scans and MRIs with snatches of Celine Dion and Stravinsky as they reported on the biological foundations of music. Several lines of evidence suggest that the human brain is wired for music, and that some forms of intelligence are enhanced by music. **Perhaps the most striking hint that the brain holds a special place in its gray matter for music is that people can typically remember scores of tunes, and recognize hundreds more. But we can recall only snatches of a few prose passages ("Four score and seven years ago . . .").** Also, music affects the mind in powerful ways: it not only incites passion, belligerence, serenity or fear, but does so even in people who do not know from experience, for instance, that a particular crescendo means the killer is about to pop out on the movie screen. All in all, says psychologist Isabelle Peretz of the University of Montreal, "the brain seems to be specialized for music."

—Sharon Begley, "Music on the Mind,"
Newsweek, July 24, 2000, p. 51

20-2: Integrating and Citing Sources within Your Paper

When using information you have gathered from other sources, you may want to use direct quotes, indirect quotes, summaries, or paraphrases. You also need to make sure that you do not plagiarize (use the author's exact words without using quotation marks and/or referencing the source). Using the following passage, write on separate paper or your computer a one-sentence summary of the entire passage, a paraphrase of the part of the passage that is in bold type, and a direct quote that could be used in a research essay about feng shui. (Be sure to introduce the quote with a signal phrase.) At the end of your summary, paraphrase, or quote, include a parenthetical reference to the original source.

ORIGINAL SOURCE

Feng shui, for those who have somehow missed its myriad references in pop culture, means wind and water in Chinese. **The 3,500-year-old system, once used only by China's Emperor, is based on the idea that landscapes, buildings and even whole cities have hidden zones of energy (*qi*), which can be manipulated by the shape, size and color of a structure as well as its entrances. A building that allows *qi* to flow freely is said to have good feng shui, which brings prosperity and success.**

—Ajay Singh, "Luck Be a Stone Lion,"
Time, July 3, 2000, p. 53

20-3: Integrating and Citing Sources within Your Paper

When using information you have gathered from other sources, you may want to use direct quotes, indirect quotes, summaries, or paraphrases. You also need to make sure that you do not plagiarize (use the author's exact words without using quotation marks and/or referencing the source). Using the following passage, write on separate paper or your computer a one-sentence summary of the entire passage, a paraphrase of the part of the passage that is in bold type, and a direct quote that could be used in a research essay on whether or not competition in children's games and sports is productive. (Be sure to introduce the quote with a signal phrase.) At the end of your summary, paraphrase, or quote, include a parenthetical reference to the original source.

ORIGINAL SOURCE

Competition leads children to envy winners, to dismiss losers (there's no nastier epithet in our language than "Loser!") and to be suspicious of just about everyone. **Competition makes it difficult to regard others as potential friends or collaborators; even if you're not my rival today, you could be tomorrow.**

This is not to say that competitors will always detest each other. But trying to outdo someone is not conducive to trust—indeed, it would be irrational to trust someone who gains from your failure. At best, competition leads one to look at others through narrowed eyes; at worst, it invites outright aggression. Existing relationships are strained to the breaking point, while new friendships are often nipped in the bud.

—Alfie Kohn, "The Case against Competition"

The entire essay "The Case against Competition" by Alfie Kohn is printed in Chapter 51 of *Real Essays with Readings.*

20-4: Integrating and Citing Sources within Your Paper

When using information you have gathered from other sources, you may want to use direct quotes, indirect quotes, summaries, or paraphrases. You also need to make sure that you do not plagiarize (use the author's exact words without using quotation marks and/or referencing the source). Using the following passage, write on separate paper or your computer a one-sentence summary of the entire passage, a paraphrase of the part of the passage that is in bold type, and a direct quote that could be used in a research essay about stereotypes. (Be sure to introduce the quote with a signal phrase.) At the end of your summary, paraphrase, or quote, include a parenthetical reference to the original source.

ORIGINAL SOURCE

Why is it that we stereotype the world in such irrational and harmful fashion? In part, we begin to typecast people in our childhood years. **Early in life, as every parent whose child has watched a TV Western knows, we learn to spot the Good Guys from the Bad Guys.** Some years ago, a social psychologist showed very clearly how powerful these stereotypes of childhood vision are. He secretly asked the most popular youngsters in an elementary school to make errors in their morning gym exercises. Afterwards, he asked the class if anyone had noticed any mistakes during gym period. Oh, yes, said the children. But it was the *unpopular* members of the class—the "bad guys"—they remembered as being out of step.

We not only grow up with standardized pictures forming inside of us, but as grown-ups we are constantly having them thrust upon us. Some of them, like the half-joking, half-serious stereotypes of mothers-in-law, or country yokels, or psychiatrists, are dinned into us by the stock jokes we hear and repeat. In fact, without such stereotypes, there would be a lot fewer jokes. Still other stereotypes are perpetuated by the advertisements we read, the movies we see, the books we read.

—Robert L. Heilbroner, "Don't Let Stereotypes Warp Your Judgments"

The entire essay "Don't Let Stereotypes Warp Your Judgments" by Robert L. Heilbroner is printed in Chapter 50 of *Real Essays with Readings*.

20-5: **Integrating and Citing Sources within Your Paper**

When using information you have gathered from other sources, you may want to use direct quotes, indirect quotes, summaries, or paraphrases. You also need to make sure that you do not plagiarize (use the author's exact words without using quotation marks and/or referencing the source). Using the following passage, write on separate paper or your computer a one-sentence summary of the entire passage, a paraphrase of the part of the passage that is in bold type, and a direct quote that could be used in a research essay about TV addiction. (Be sure to introduce the quote with a signal phrase.) At the end of your summary, paraphrase, or quote, include a parenthetical reference to the original source.

ORIGINAL SOURCE

Self-confessed television addicts often feel they "ought" to do other things—but the fact that they don't read and don't plant their garden or sew or crochet or play games or have conversations means that those activities are no longer as desirable as television viewing. In a way, the lives of heavy viewers are as unbalanced by their television "habit" as drug addicts' or alcoholics' lives. **They are living in a holding pattern, as it were, passing up the activities that lead to growth or development or a sense of accomplishment.** This is one reason people talk about their television viewing so ruefully, so apologetically. They are aware that it is an unproductive experience, that by any human measure almost any other endeavor is more worthwhile.

—Marie Winn, "Cookies or Heroin?"

The entire essay "Cookies or Heroin?" by Marie Winn is printed in Chapter 48 of *Real Essays with Readings.*

Answer Key

Answers to Exercises 20-1 through 20-5 will vary depending on what passages the student selects. Possible answers are given below.

Answers to 20-1

Possible answers:

SUMMARY

Recent scientific findings suggest that the human brain is preprogrammed for music (Begley 51).

PARAPHRASE

Humans can store a large number of songs in their memory; however, people rarely remember more than a few sentences of written material (Begley 51).

DIRECT QUOTE

As Begley states, "several lines of evidence suggest that the human brain is wired for music" (Begley 51).

Answers to 20-2

Possible answers:

SUMMARY

Feng shui, an ancient Chinese method of designing and organizing spaces, is said to maximize energy and bring wealth (Singh 53).

PARAPHRASE

Feng shui relies on *qi*, energy that can be affected by a space's character—its shape and dimensions. A building with good feng shui, which allows *qi* to move freely throughout a space, rewards its owner with worldly success (Singh 53).

DIRECT QUOTE

As Singh states, "A building that allows *qi* to flow freely is said to have good feng shui" (53).

Answers to 20-3

Possible answers:

SUMMARY

Because it teaches them distrust and rivalry, competition damages childrens' relationships with each other (Kohn 705).

PARAPHRASE

Everyone is a current or potential rival in a competitive environment, making it hard to create friendships (Kohn 705).

DIRECT QUOTE

As Kohn states, "At best, competition leads one to look at others through narrowed eyes; at worst, it invites outright aggression" (705).

Answers to 20-4

Possible answers:

SUMMARY

Stereotypes, which we begin to learn as children, are perpetuated by jokes and the media (Heilbroner 693).

PARAPHRASE

We begin to use stereotypes as children, when stories—such as those in TV Westerns—teach us to distinguish "good" characters from "bad" ones (Heilbroner 693).

DIRECT QUOTE

According to Heilbroner, "We not only grow up with standardized pictures forming inside of us, but as grown-ups we are constantly having them thrust upon us" (693).

Answers to 20-5

Possible answers:

SUMMARY

Television addicts, like drug addicts or alcoholics, often realize that their addiction is keeping them from participating in healthier, more productive activities (Winn 674–75).

PARAPHRASE

Because television addicts would rather watch TV than participate in more fulfilling activities, their lives are not productively moving forward (Winn 674–75).

DIRECT QUOTE

"In a way," states Winn, "the lives of heavy viewers are as unbalanced by their television 'habit' as drug addicts' or alcoholics'" (674–75).

Diagnostic Tests for Editing Skills
(*Chapters 22–41*)

Diagnostic Test–A

Sentence Completeness

In the blank, write "RO" for run-on (two sentences joined incorrectly), "F" for fragment (incomplete sentence), and "S" for complete sentence.

_____ 1. Because the language barrier is the greatest obstacle that I have faced since I have been living in this country.

_____ 2. My employer made me do just about everything at once, such as running the cash register, taking orders, and preparing food.

_____ 3. Always go to dinner after my night class.

_____ 4. College is not just educational, it also makes you feel better about yourself.

_____ 5. That was the first show in which I didn't win an award for sculpture I was still proud of my hard work.

_____ 6. I remember the first day of school; I couldn't speak English very well and had a lot of trouble with my classes.

_____ 7. For example, spending your last few dollars on a lottery ticket.

_____ 8. I also feel more mature by handling responsibilities at home—for example, helping my parents out by paying bills, cleaning house, and taking care of my brother.

_____ 9. Which in turn made me and the customers mad.

_____ 10. Although my landlord lives right above me, is hard to find when I need him.

_____ 11. At UPS, the atmosphere is very different everybody runs around yelling and screaming about one thing or another.

_____ 12. They work outside the house, when they come back home, they still have to take care of the children and be responsible for their comfort, school, and clothes.

Misplaced and Dangling Modifiers

Edit the following sentences to correct errors with dangling or misplaced modifiers.

13. Opening the envelope, a check fell out into her hands.

14. Fran and Albert decided to hang the painting in the den with the African jungle scene.

15. In the middle of the test, Keith discovered that he could only answer ten of the fifty questions.

16. The mothers dressed their babies to protect them from bad weather in snowsuits.

17. After throwing a red towel into the washing machine, Troy's T-shirts turned pink.

Correct Word Choice, Verbs, Modifiers

Circle the correct word or words in parentheses.

18. Today, women (has, have) a lot of opportunities to get better jobs.

19. I hope the man I marry someday treats me as (good, well) as my father treats my mother.

20. I want to take (a, the) computer class that you recommended yesterday.

21. The stationary bicycle and the treadmill are excellent exercise machines to help an older person improve (his, his or her, their) fitness.

22. I had never thought it possible to be in the honor society because of the obstacles that (lay, lied) in my way.

23. Combat troops are tough, heartless, dirty, and (smell, smelly).

24. As the doctor entered the emergency room, the patient (asks, asked) for assistance.

25. My sister had difficulty (scheduling, to schedule) personal appointments during her hectic work week.

26. The (rapid, rapidly) moving car ran the red light and hit the bus.

27. At sixty-eight, he has experienced the pain and agony that (comes, come) from having two heart attacks.

28. There should be no limitations placed on people because of (his, his or her, their) gender.

29. When I told her the position was no longer available, she sounded (disappointed, bummed out).

30. (Due to the fact that, Because) she had to stop by the day-care center, Amanda missed the first ten minutes of class.

31. I get the majority of my information from newspapers and from (watching television, television).

32. There (is, are) several reasons to finish your homework before class.

33. The child behaved (bad, badly) when his mother told him he couldn't have any ice cream.

34. The government agency announced that (it, they) would refund money to anyone who had the proper documents.

35. The weather this winter seems (cold, colder) than it was last year.

36. Dr. Percy (has spoke, has spoken) at our nursing club's awards banquet for the past three years.

37. Being able to use the computers (has, have) improved my writing skills.

38. After Charlie changed the engine, the Corvette was (faster, fastest, more fast) than the Mustang.

39. The coach named Sebastian and (he, him) to the all-star team.

40. The Writing Center tutor told us that we are each responsible (about, for) our own disks.

Punctuation and Capitalization

Add the correct punctuation and capitalization in the following sentences.

41. The family will spend christmas in san juan this december.

42. Where are you going? John asked Tran.

43. We will need the following supplies a three-ring notebook, notebook paper, a pen, and a red pencil.

44. If you dont want to go swimming, you wont need to pay a fee because its not required by the state.

45. Luisa who enjoys Tejana music volunteered to find a band for the school dance.

46. We elected Sue, president, Bill, vice-president, Quinn, treasurer, and Sam, secretary.

47. in american literature, professor martinez asked us to read the novel *the old man and the sea.*

48. Although both cars are very fast the Mustang has a V-8, 289 carburetor.

49. With the lottery, people buy tickets by choice therefore, they are not forced to spend money they do not have.

50. Theres no way to determine if theyre receiving assistance on the project.

51. The students who studied made excellent grades on their tests the others were not satisfied with their grades.

52. During the long holiday weekend we are planning to mow the yard clean the house go to the lake and see a movie.

53. Fellow citizens, the president announced, the events of today will be re-membered for many years.

54. Although we had a substitute teacher we still had to take a test and we had to write a paragraph before we could leave class.

55. The smith family moved to 925 henderson lane in albany, new york.

Spelling

Correct any spelling errors. Put "C" in the blank if you see no error.

_____ 56. Three hundred dollars is alot of money.

_____ 57. The doctors were egar to help my father.

_____ 58. An on-campus day care offers convience.

_____ 59. Don't embarass me.

_____ 60. We past the same park three times.

_____ 61. Who's car is parked in the driveway?

_____ 62. It was a solemn ocassion.

_____ 63. Did the child brake his arm?

_____ 64. John enjoyed writting.

_____ 65. My opinon is always right.

_____ 66. Amy will pursue a law degree.

_____ 67. I enjoy the peace and quite.

_____ 68. It was a common occurrence.

_____ 69. That cat can preform tricks.

_____ 70. Cars are taxed according to their wieght.

Diagnostic Test–A: Answer Key

Sentence Completeness

1. F 2. S 3. F 4. RO 5. RO 6. S 7. F 8. S 9. F 10. F 11. RO 12. RO

Misplaced and Dangling Modifiers

Possible edits shown.

13. When Alice opened the envelope, a check fell out into her hands.
14. Fran and Albert decided to hang the painting with the African jungle scene in the den.
15. In the middle of the test, Keith discovered that he could answer only ten of the fifty questions.
16. To protect them from bad weather, the mothers dressed their babies in snowsuits.
17. After he threw a red towel into the washing machine, Troy's T-shirts turned pink.

Correct Word Choice, Verbs, Modifiers

18. have   19. well   20. the   21. his or her   22. lay   23. smelly
24. asked   25. scheduling   26. rapidly   27. come   28. their
29. disappointed   30. Because   31. television   32. are   33. badly
34. it   35. colder   36. has spoken   37. has   38. faster   39. him
40. for

Punctuation and Capitalization

Edits shown.

41. The family will spend **C**hristmas in **S**an **J**uan this **D**ecember.
42. "Where are you going?" John asked Tran.
43. We will need the following supplies: a three-ring notebook**,** notebook paper, a pen, and a red pencil.
44. If you **don't** want to go swimming, you **won't** need to pay a fee because **it's** not required by the state.
45. Luisa**,** who enjoys Tejana music, volunteered to find a band for the school dance.
46. We elected Sue, president**;** Bill, vice-president**;** Quinn, treasurer**;** and Sam, secretary.
47. **I**n American **L**iterature, **P**rofessor **M**artinez asked us to read the novel *The Old Man and the Sea.*

48. Although both cars are very fast, the Mustang has a V-8, 289 carburetor.

49. With the lottery, people buy tickets by choice; therefore, they are not forced to spend money they do not have.

50. **There's** no way to determine if **they're** receiving assistance on the project.

51. The students who studied made excellent grades on their tests; the others were not satisfied with their grades.

52. During the long holiday weekend, we are planning to mow the yard, clean the house, go to the lake, and see a movie.

53. "Fellow citizens," the president announced, "the events of today will be remembered for many years."

54. Although we had a substitute teacher, we still had to take a test, and we had to write a paragraph before we could leave class.

55. The **S**mith family moved to 925 **H**enderson **L**ane in **A**lbany, **N**ew **Y**ork.

Spelling

56. a lot   57. eager   58. convenience   59. embarrass   60. passed   61. Whose
62. occasion   63. break   64. writing   65. opinion   66. C   67. quiet   68. C
69. perform   70. weight

Diagnostic Test–A

Identification of Problem Areas

The following table will help you identify your students' strengths and weaknesses in grammar, sentence structure, punctuation, and spelling skills. Use the table to match chapter content in *Real Essays* with individual items from the diagnostic test.

Chapter in Real Essays	*Test Items*
23 Fragments	1, 3, 7, 9, 10
24 Run-ons	4, 5, 11, 12
25 Problems with subject-verb agreement	18, 27, 32, 37
26 Verb problems	22, 24, 36
27 Pronouns	21, 28, 34, 39
28 Adjectives and adverbs	19, 26, 33, 35, 38
29 Misplaced and dangling modifiers	13, 14, 15, 16, 17
30 Coordination and subordination	48, 51, 54
31 Parallelism	23, 31
33 ESL	3, 10, 20, 25, 40
34 Word choice	29, 30
35 Commonly confused words	60, 61, 63, 67
36 Spelling	56, 57, 58, 59, 62, 64, 65, 69, 70
37 Commas	45, 52, 54
38 Apostrophes	44, 50
39 Quotation marks	42, 53
40 Other punctuation	43, 46, 49, 51
41 Capitalization	41, 47, 55

Diagnostic Test–B

Part One

Each of the following sentences has boldface sections labeled **A** and **B**. Read each sentence carefully, looking for errors in grammar, punctuation, or spelling. If you find an error in any of the boldface sections, write the letter of the problem area in the space provided. If there is no error, write the letter "C" in the space provided.

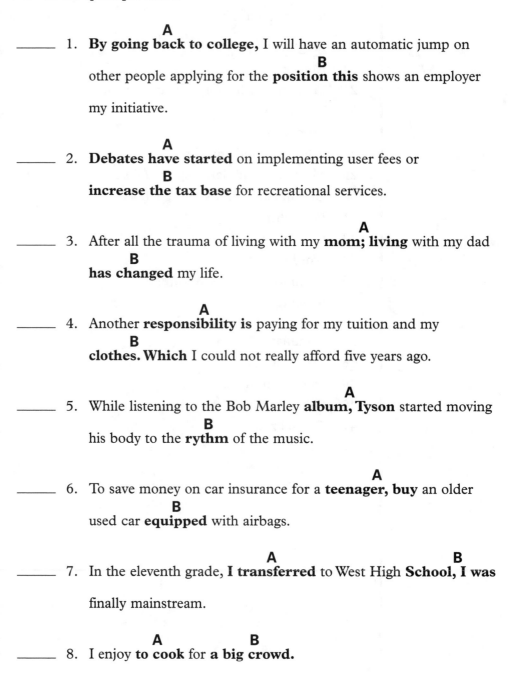

_____ 1. **By going back to college,** I will have an automatic jump on
other people applying for the **position this** shows an employer
my initiative.

_____ 2. **Debates have started** on implementing user fees or
increase the tax base for recreational services.

_____ 3. After all the trauma of living with my **mom; living** with my dad
has changed my life.

_____ 4. Another **responsibility is** paying for my tuition and my
clothes. Which I could not really afford five years ago.

_____ 5. While listening to the Bob Marley **album, Tyson** started moving
his body to the **rythm** of the music.

_____ 6. To save money on car insurance for a **teenager, buy** an older
used car **equipped** with airbags.

_____ 7. In the eleventh grade, **I transferred** to West High **School, I was**
finally mainstream.

_____ 8. I enjoy **to cook** for **a big crowd.**

                                    A   **B**

_____ 9. If a family **member disagrees** with a **doctor's choices,** who

wins?

                          A   **B**

_____ 10. Travel **games, such** as Battleship, **provides** several hours of fun

for children when you are traveling long distances in your car.

                                                A

_____ 11. The United States will be stronger in the **future; if** it helps all

B

children **receive** education and medical care.

                           A

_____ 12. A **family's** insurance policy may not cover medical expenses

B

when students are away from their **parents** home area.

                                   A

_____ 13. See if you can buy insurance **direct** from the college, since some

B

schools make coverage available for **their** students.

                         A   **B**

_____ 14. **Is difficult** to imagine **myself designing** my own Web page.

                                              A

_____ 15. Stan Weston, creator of G. I. Joe action figures, **advises,**

"You don't have to be a genius to make a living with your

B

imagination".

                                            A

_____ 16. My dad did both jobs when my mom was **working, he** cooked

B

for us and took care of **my sisters and me** when we were sick.

_____ 17. The best time to water lawns is between 4:00 A.M. and

                         A   **B**

8:00 A.M. but if that's too early for **you, water** between

8:00 A.M. and noon.

                         A

_____ 18. We must **decide if** saving a life is more important than saving

B

the **countries money.**

_____ 19.   My **Mother** prefers to drive ten miles out of her **way in order**

to avoid driving on the freeway.

_____ 20.   A college education **will help me** find a job in the field

that I like. After I earn my degree in accounting.

_____ 21.   To avoid traffic **tickets, you** need to obey all the

rules and visual cues: speed limits, red lights, and stop signs.

_____ 22.   When he dropped the letter in the mailbox, Joe **realized** that he

had wrote the check for the wrong amount.

_____ 23.   A federal law **gives** employers the right to monitor all electronic

messages stored on **its** system.

_____ 24.   Many people believe that it will take **goverment** intervention to

stem the rising cost of medical **care, including** doctor visits,

prescriptions, and hospital stays.

_____ 25.   My dad was always there when I needed someone to

talk to. Unlike my mom, who would **act like she didn't have**

time to listen to my problems.

_____ 26.   For **valentine's day,** I'm planning a **February** cruise to

Jamaica.

_____ 27.   After the bee **stang** the baby, his arm swelled **tremendously.**

Part Two

In each of the following sentences, decide which of the words in parentheses is the correct choice for that sentence. Then write the letter indicating the correct word in the space provided.

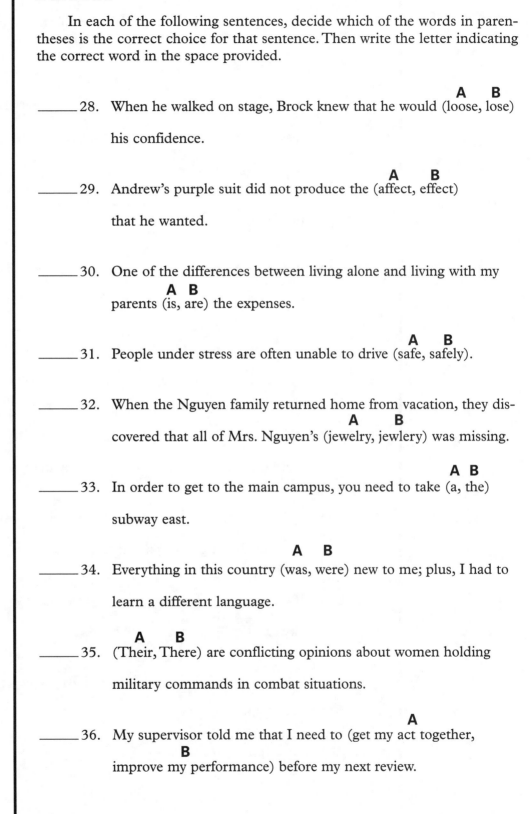

_____ 28. When he walked on stage, Brock knew that he would (loose, lose) his confidence.

                      A **B**

_____ 29. Andrew's purple suit did not produce the (affect, effect) that he wanted.

_____ 30. One of the differences between living alone and living with my parents (is, are) the expenses.

_____ 31. People under stress are often unable to drive (safe, safely).

_____ 32. When the Nguyen family returned home from vacation, they discovered that all of Mrs. Nguyen's (jewelry, jewlery) was missing.

_____ 33. In order to get to the main campus, you need to take (a, the) subway east.

_____ 34. Everything in this country (was, were) new to me; plus, I had to learn a different language.

_____ 35. (Their, There) are conflicting opinions about women holding military commands in combat situations.

_____ 36. My supervisor told me that I need to (get my act together, improve my performance) before my next review.

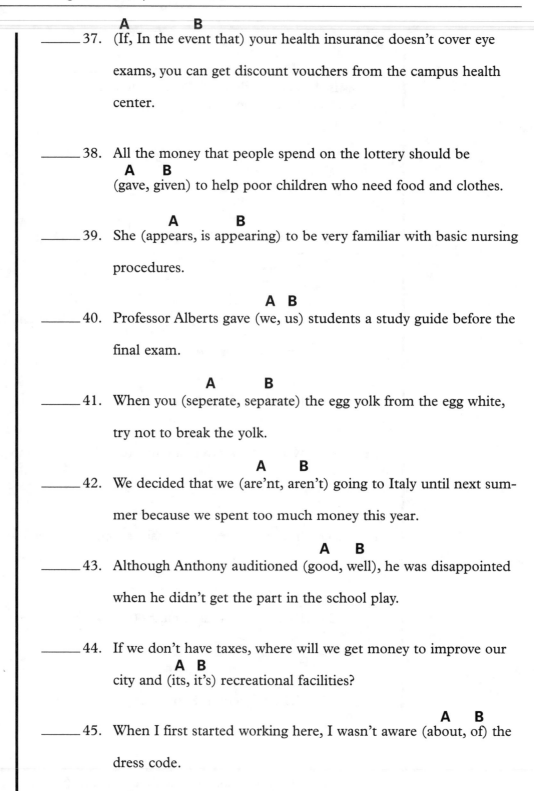

              A   **B**

_____ 37. (If, In the event that) your health insurance doesn't cover eye exams, you can get discount vouchers from the campus health center.

_____ 38. All the money that people spend on the lottery should be
A   **B**
(gave, given) to help poor children who need food and clothes.

                A   **B**

_____ 39. She (appears, is appearing) to be very familiar with basic nursing procedures.

                         A B

_____ 40. Professor Alberts gave (we, us) students a study guide before the final exam.

               A   **B**

_____ 41. When you (seperate, separate) the egg yolk from the egg white, try not to break the yolk.

                   A   **B**

_____ 42. We decided that we (are'nt, aren't) going to Italy until next summer because we spent too much money this year.

                      A B

_____ 43. Although Anthony auditioned (good, well), he was disappointed when he didn't get the part in the school play.

_____ 44. If we don't have taxes, where will we get money to improve our
        A B
city and (its, it's) recreational facilities?

                            A   **B**

_____ 45. When I first started working here, I wasn't aware (about, of) the dress code.

Part Three

For each number, choose the sentence that is correctly worded and punctuated. Write the letter indicating the correct sentence in the space provided.

_____ 46. **A.** Men and women, who eat high levels of margarine, are at higher risk than those who eat less.

B. Men and women who eat high levels of margarine are at higher risk than those who eat less.

_____ 47. **A.** Women are deciding to be construction workers rather than secretaries.

B. Women are deciding to be construction workers rather than being a secretary.

_____ 48. **A.** Not only do tax-funded recreational facilities help communities as a whole, but it also helps each individual.

B. Not only do tax-funded recreational facilities help communities as a whole, but they also help each individual.

_____ 49. **A.** Five years from now I will get a bachelor's degree; and I will become a teacher.

B. Five years from now I will get a bachelor's degree, and I will become a teacher.

_____ 50. **A.** Therefore, after I go to college, the world is mine.

B. Therefore, after going to college, the world is mine.

_____ 51. **A.** During her first semester in college, Cam took Reading, English, History, and Math.

B. Cam took reading, English, history, and math during her first semester in college.

_____ 52. **A.** I would much rather call than sitting down and writing a letter.

B. I would much rather call than sit down and write a letter.

_____ 53. **A.** My sister always has a plan and sticks to it, while I often do things at the last minute or change my plans.

B. My sister always has a plan and sticks to it, while, I often do things at the last minute or change my plans.

_____ 54. **A.** This job was stressful because if I do not put the belt on correctly, I will probably ruin the engine.

B. This job was stressful because if I did not put the belt on correctly, I probably would have ruined the engine.

_____ 55. **A.** "Don't belittle your child's fears," says Dr. Leah Klungness, school psychologist, "or he will not discuss them with you."

B. "Don't belittle your child's fears", says Dr. Leah Klungness, school psychologist, "Or he will not discuss them with you".

_____ 56. **A.** Female athletes suffer eight times more knee injuries than male athletes; however, they can avoid injuries if they strengthen their hamstrings by jumping rope for a few minutes three times a week.

B. Female athletes suffer eight times more knee injuries than male athletes, however, they can avoid injuries if they strengthen their hamstrings by jumping rope for a few minutes three times a week.

_____ 57. **A.** You can keep deer and rabbits out of your garden with a homemade repellent: two tablespoons of hot pepper sauce, one gallon of water, and a tablespoon of nondetergent dish soap.

B. You can keep deer and rabbits out of your garden with a homemade repellent, two tablespoons of hot pepper sauce, one gallon of water, and a tablespoon of nondetergent dish soap.

_____ 58. **A.** Working on a computer is no more damaging to the eyes than paperwork or any other close-up labor.

B. Working on a computer is no more damaging to the eyes than doing paperwork or any other close-up labor.

_____ 59. **A.** Doctors, not families, should determine a patient's treatment because the doctors are the ones with the professional degrees and years of experience.

B. Doctors, not families, should determine a patient's treatment; because, the doctors are the ones with the professional degrees and years of experience.

_____ 60. **A.** "Why am I feeling so angry?" Jonathan asked his counselor.

B. "Why am I feeling so angry?", Jonathan asked his counselor.

_____ 61. **A.** All children deserve the best education, and the best medical care they can get.

B. All children deserve the best education and the best medical care they can get.

_____ 62. **A.** Rosemary almost walks to work every day.

B. Rosemary walks to work almost every day.

_____ 63. **A.** The professor told Sasha and I that we had the highest grades in the class.

B. The professor told Sasha and me that we had the highest grades in the class.

_____ 64. **A.** Physical play, drawing, painting, and small tasks help children master their world and can make them less fearful.

B. Physical play, drawing, painting, and doing small tasks help children master their world and can make them less fearful.

_____ 65. **A.** The television news reported a huge fire near the campus as I was waiting for my ride to school.

B. Waiting for my ride to school, the television news reported a huge fire near the campus.

Diagnostic Test–B: Answer Key

1. B	18. B	35. B	52. B
2. B	19. A	36. B	53. A
3. A	20. B	37. A	54. B
4. B	21. C	38. B	55. A
5. B	22. B	39. A	56. A
6. C	23. B	40. B	57. A
7. B	24. A	41. B	58. B
8. A	25. A	42. B	59. A
9. C	26. A	43. B	60. A
10. B	27. A	44. A	61. B
11. A	28. B	45. B	62. B
12. B	29. B	46. B	63. B
13. A	30. A	47. A	64. B
14. A	31. B	48. B	65. A
15. B	32. A	49. B	
16. A	33. B	50. A	
17. A	34. A	51. B	

Diagnostic Test–B

Identification of Problem Areas

The following table will help you identify your students' strengths and weaknesses in grammar, sentence structure, punctuation, and spelling skills. Use the table to match chapter content in *Real Essays* with individual items from the diagnostic test.

Chapter in Real Essays		*Test Items*
23	Fragments	4, 20, 25
24	Run-ons	1, 7, 16, 56
25	Problems with subject–verb agreement	10, 30, 34
26	Verb problems	22, 27, 38, 54
27	Pronouns	23, 40, 48, 63
28	Adjectives and adverbs	13, 31, 43
29	Misplaced and dangling modifiers	50, 62, 65
30	Coordination and subordination	3, 11, 17, 59
31	Parallelism	2, 47, 52, 58, 64
33	ESL	8, 14, 33, 39, 45
34	Word choice	36, 37
35	Commonly confused words	28, 29, 35, 44
36	Spelling	5, 24, 32, 41
37	Commas	1, 17, 46, 49, 53, 61
38	Apostrophes	9, 12, 18, 42
39	Quotation marks	15, 55, 60
40	Other punctuation	3, 11, 21, 57, 59
41	Capitalization	19, 26, 51, 55

Diagnostic Test–C

Sentence Completeness

In the blank, write "RO" for run-on (two sentences joined incorrectly), "F" for fragment (incomplete sentence), and "S" for complete sentence.

_____ 1. To get through college as quickly as possible.

_____ 2. Although the hours are long and the pay is mediocre.

_____ 3. The Internet has made it easier for students to buy term papers and pass them off as their own work.

_____ 4. Household chores never really end they just go on and on.

_____ 5. Debbie wants to buy a greyhound, however, the landlord does not allow pets.

_____ 6. Since the Beatles, the Rolling Stones, and other British groups "invaded" America in the 1960s.

_____ 7. If you own a home, you can deduct expenses from your tax return, there's no such allowance for those of us who rent.

_____ 8. A computer allows a doctor to monitor the vital signs of a fetus and its mother without being in the same room.

_____ 9. A pencil is more useful than a yellow highlighter, the pencil allows you to jot down comments and questions in the margins of the page.

_____ 10. Some foods believed to reduce the risk of cancer.

_____ 11. The bus offers a quicker, more direct way to reach my apartment, but it does not run as often as the subway train.

_____ 12. In the beginning of the summer, and again at the end of summer.

Misplaced and Dangling Modifiers

Edit the following sentences to correct errors with dangling or misplaced modifiers.

13. Lacking strong math skills, the course was too difficult.

14. The parts of the book are left out of the film that Liza found most interesting to read.

15. Several months behind in their rent payments, the landlord insisted that Jenny and Steve find a new place to live.

16. After sleeping in it, the cat's basket was covered with a thick layer of fur.

17. Martha nearly meets with each of her clients every week.

Correct Word Choice, Verbs, Modifiers

Circle the correct word or words in the parentheses.

18. Prozac is the best known of the newer drugs that (fight, fights) depression with only minor side effects.

19. Students who own computers have an advantage over (his or her, their) classmates.

20. Monica met with colleagues, spoke with her supervisor, and (discussed her concerns, her concerns were discussed) with friends before asking for a transfer.

21. Investing your money in overseas markets (is, are) often riskier than buying U.S. stocks.

22. Tim avoids (to buy, buying) fruits and vegetables that are not organically grown.

23. Trish did (good, well) in her management course, which had only eight students and an energetic professor.

24. (It is the opinion of many Americans, Many Americans believe) that the death penalty gives murderers what they deserve.

25. Although the plot was slow, the film was photographed (beautiful, beautifully).

26. Some people can sleep on an airplane, but I have to be (laying, lying) down.

27. (A, The) classroom that my business class meets in has a noisy heating system.

28. After Pam lifted up a large rock from the tide pool, she (discovers, discovered) an unusual species of hermit crab.

29. In my neighborhood, unemployment is (worse, worst) today than when my parents were young.

30. According to psychologist Joel D. Block, a typical friendship between men (has, have) less emotional depth than a friendship between women.

31. Darlene wants to build her new home near the (green large, large green) hills at the edge of town.

32. I am (psyched, excited) to be offered one of your paid internships.

33. Should the school year for elementary, middle, and high school students last (long, longer) than nine months?

34. The university offers health insurance only to (its, their) full-time employees.

35. One problem with portable phones (occur, occurs) when you can't find the receiver.

36. Li Zhen was proud (for, of) the improvements she made in her spoken and written English.

37. It is important to use up a supply of antibiotics even if the infection appears to have (gone, went) away.

38. Many scientists believe that severe storms are occurring (more frequent, more frequently) because of global warming.

39. We can use our money either to repair the porch or (for buying, to buy) a new dining-room table.

40. A doctor shouldn't claim to always know exactly what is best for (his, his or her, their) patients.

Punctuation and Capitalization

Add the correct punctuation and capitalization to the following sentences.

41. Mount Rainier which is near Seattle has taken the lives of a lot of mountain climbers.

42. My italian grandparents arrived in san pedro, near los angeles, around the time of world war I.

43. Two friends are majoring in economics and international relations and Justin is interested in these subjects himself.

44. When she broke the school record in the quarter-mile, Kate said, This is the most satisfying thing I've ever done!

45. The childrens room at the library is colorfully decorated.

46. Writers revise their drafts by emphasizing key ideas removing unneeded information and paying special attention to clarity.

47. Is it still possible for me to get into this course? Nathan asked, but the professor shook his head.

48. Kevin wouldnt have applied for the job if he didnt think he was qualified.

49. Don't stop now there are only two weeks left in the semester.

50. I must do three things before the end of the month pay the rent have the brakes checked on the Toyota and meet with the career counselor.

51. Centuries ago, latin was the international language of europe, just as english is today.

52. A professor whos sensitive to students feelings will earn the students respect.

53. Theresa was disappointed by her grade on her essay she went to see the professor to ask if she could revise it.

54. Julian a teammate of mine in high school is transferring to this college.

55. As anyone who has met him already knows Jim is an extremely smart guy.

Spelling

Correct any spelling errors. Put "C" in the blank if you see no error.

_____ 56. Rosana has the necesary skills.

_____ 57. This software is a definate improvement.

_____ 58. Their is nothing wrong with my eyesight.

_____ 59. My score was higher then hers.

_____ 60. Kim use to work in an automotive shop.

_____ 61. The fly got traped in the spider's web.

_____ 62. We recieve our grades in the mail.

_____ 63. This arguement could go on forever.

_____ 64. Separate the paper from the glass.

_____ 65. Promise not to deceive me.

_____ 66. She made a valueable contribution.

_____ 67. He should have taken the orignal offer.

_____ 68. I have acheived all of my goals.

_____ 69. The bull got lose from its pen.

_____ 70. It's time to protect the enviroment.

Diagnostic Test–C: Answer Key

Sentence Completeness

1. F   2. F   3. S   4. RO   5. RO   6. F   7. RO   8. S   9. RO   10. F   11. S   12. F

Misplaced and Dangling Modifiers

Possible edits shown.

13. Because he lacked strong math skills, the course was too difficult for him.
14. The parts of the book that Liza found most interesting to read are left out of the film.
15. The landlord insisted that Jenny and Steve, who were several months behind in their rent payments, find a new place to live.
16. After the cat slept in it, the basket was covered with a thick layer of fur.
17. Martha meets with each of her clients nearly every week.

Correct Word Choice, Verbs, Modifiers

18. fight   19. their   20. discussed her concerns   21. is   22. buying
23. well   24. Many Americans believe   25. beautifully   26. lying   27. The
28. discovered   29. worse   30. has   31. large green   32. excited   33. longer
34. its   35. occurs   36. of   37. gone   38. more frequently   39. to buy
40. his or her

Punctuation and Capitalization

Edits shown.

41. Mount Rainier**,** which is near Seattle**,** has taken the lives of a lot of mountain climbers.
42. My **I**talian grandparents arrived in **S**an **P**edro, near **L**os **A**ngeles, around the time of **W**orld **W**ar I.
43. Two friends are majoring in economics and international relations**,** and Justin is interested in these subjects himself.
44. When she broke the school record in the quarter-mile, Kate said, **"**This is the most satisfying thing I've ever done!**"**
45. The children**'**s room at the library is colorfully decorated.
46. Writers revise their drafts by emphasizing key ideas**,** removing unneeded information**,** and paying special attention to clarity.
47. **"**Is it still possible for me to get into this course?**"** Nathan asked, but the professor shook his head.

48. Kevin **wouldn't** have applied for the job if he **didn't** think he was qualified.

49. Don't stop now. **T**here are only two weeks left in the semester.

50. I must do three things before the end of the month**:** pay the rent, have the brakes checked on the Toyota, and meet with the career counselor.

51. Centuries ago, **L**atin was the international language of **E**urope, just as English is today.

52. A professor **who's** sensitive to **students'** feelings will earn the **students'** respect.

53. Theresa was disappointed by her grade on her essay. **S**he went to see the professor to ask if she could revise it.

54. Julian**,** a teammate of mine in high school**,** is transferring to this college.

55. As anyone who has met him already knows, Jim is an extremely smart guy.

Spelling

56. necessary   57. definite   58. There   59. than   60. used   61. trapped
62. receive   63. argument   64. C   65. C   66. valuable   67. original
68. achieved   69. loose   70. environment

Diagnostic Test–C

Identification of Problem Areas

The following table will help you to identify your students' strengths and weaknesses in grammar, sentence structure, punctuation, and spelling skills. Use the table to match chapter content in *Real Essays* with individual items from the diagnostic test.

Chapter in **Real Essays**		*Test Items*
23	Fragments	1, 2, 6, 10, 12
24	Run-ons	4, 5, 7, 9, 43, 49, 53
25	Problems with subject–verb agreement	18, 21, 30, 35
26	Verb problems	26, 28, 37
27	Pronouns	19, 34, 40
28	Adjectives and adverbs	23, 25, 29, 33, 38
29	Misplaced and dangling modifiers	13, 14, 15, 16, 17
30	Coordination and subordination	41, 43, 55
31	Parallelism	20, 39
33	ESL	22, 27, 31, 36
34	Word choice	24, 32
35	Commonly confused words	58, 59, 60, 69
36	Spelling	56, 57, 61, 62, 63, 64, 65, 66, 67, 68, 70
37	Commas	41, 43, 46, 50, 54, 55
38	Apostrophes	45, 48, 52
39	Quotation marks	44, 47
40	Other punctuation	49, 50, 53
41	Capitalization	42, 51

Diagnostic Test–D

Part One

Each of the following sentences has two boldface sections labeled **A** and **B**. Read each sentence carefully, looking for errors in grammar, punctuation, and spelling. If you find an error in any of the boldfaced sections, write the letter of the problem area in the space provided. If there is no error, write the letter "C" in the space provided.

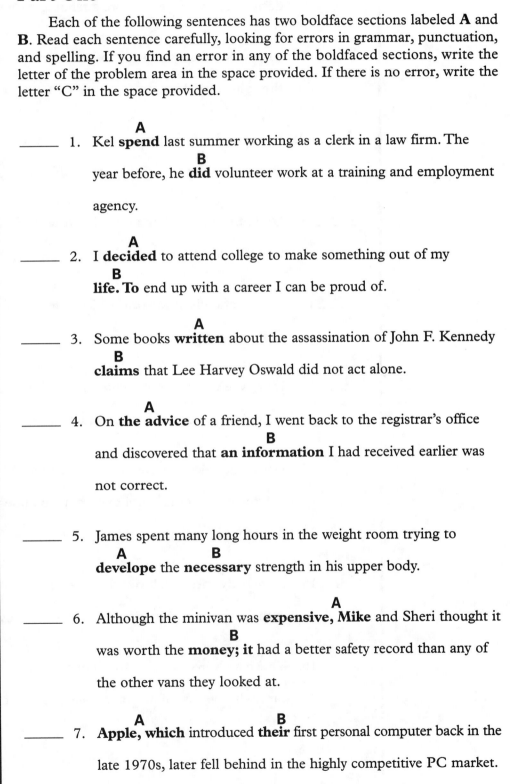

_____ 1. Kel **spend** last summer working as a clerk in a law firm. The
year before, he **did** volunteer work at a training and employment
agency.

_____ 2. I **decided** to attend college to make something out of my
life. To end up with a career I can be proud of.

_____ 3. Some books **written** about the assassination of John F. Kennedy
claims that Lee Harvey Oswald did not act alone.

_____ 4. On **the advice** of a friend, I went back to the registrar's office
and discovered that **an information** I had received earlier was
not correct.

_____ 5. James spent many long hours in the weight room trying to
develope the **necessary** strength in his upper body.

_____ 6. Although the minivan was **expensive, Mike** and Sheri thought it
was worth the **money; it** had a better safety record than any of
the other vans they looked at.

_____ 7. **Apple, which** introduced **their** first personal computer back in the
late 1970s, later fell behind in the highly competitive PC market.

_____ 8. Even though Marie graduated from high school with a high
A   **B**
grade point average and **winning** several top **awards, she**

decided to wait a year before attending college.

A   **B**
_____ 9. That was quite a **surprise** to hear about your **promotion, I**

thought it would go to someone with more experience.

A
_____ 10. Sometimes a course **is seeming** hard when you first begin, but
B
then you **realize** that it is not so difficult after all.

A   **B**
_____ 11. **One of the presidents** most important **powers is** the ability to

veto legislation passed by Congress.

A
_____ 12. Our vacation is in **March,** which is too early to enjoy the nice
B
Spring weather.

A
_____ 13. Everywhere I went in that little **town, distant** relatives of mine
B
offered me food. But I already had **ate** all I could.

A
_____ 14. Dawn and Glen are from the same city in **Illinois but** they did
B
not know each other until they came to **college; they** attended

different high schools.

A
_____ 15. If anybody tries to tell you that **it's** easy to work and go to school
B
at the same time, **they don't know what they're** talking about.

A   **B**
_____ 16. **There** are three good reasons not to own a **car, the** cost of the

car itself, the cost of insurance, and the cost of fuel and repairs.

_____ 17. You should major in something you're interested **in don't** just
^{A}
choose **something because** you've heard there are a lot of jobs
^{B}
in that field.

_____ 18. Although spring is known as the **worst time** for hay fever,
^{A}
many peoples allergies bother them in the fall, too.
^{B}

_____ 19. **That's** one of the problems with flu **shots. Sometimes** feeling
^{A} ^{B}
afterwards like you've come down with a touch of the flu.

_____ 20. Business administration is a popular **major. In** some
^{A}
cases, however, companies prefer graduates with more diverse
^{B}
backgrounds.

_____ 21. The current tax system is not entirely **fair, it's** still better than
^{A}
any of the **alternatives. Changing** to a flat tax would be a big
^{B}
mistake.

_____ 22. The reason for my **sister's** poor grades is **obvious. Too** much
^{A} ^{B}
time watching TV.

_____ 23. Jorge was reluctant to agree to the **operation, however,** the
^{A}
alternative sounded even **worse.**
^{B}

_____ 24. World Series **games which** until 1971 were played only during
^{A}
the day, now always take place at night. The games end too late
for many **fans, especially children,** to see them.
^{B}

_____ 25. **Its** about time this school did something about **its** trash problem.
^{A} ^{B}

A　　　　　　　　**B**

_____26. **Hopeing** for a lighter **sentence, the** defendant pleaded guilty to

a lesser charge.

_____27. Chandra decided to take another course from the same

A

writing teacher. Because it allowed her to save money

B

by not having to buy a different textbook.

Part Two

In each of the following sentences, decide which of the words in parentheses is the correct choice for that sentence. Then write the letter indicating the correct word or words in the space provided.

　　　　　　　　　　　　　　　　　　　A B

_____28. Familiarity with computer software programs (is, are) required

for many different types of jobs today.

　　　　　　　　　　　　A　　　**B**

_____29. I won't be able to sleep (until, untill) I finish writing this paper.

　　　　　　　A　　　**B**

_____30. Please (advice, advise) me on what courses I should take.

　　　　　　A　　　　　**B**

_____31. A (large white, white large) sign marked the entrance to the zoo.

　　　　　　　A　　　　　　**B**

_____32. Carrie (wouldnt have, wouldn't have) taken on the second job if

she didn't think she could handle it.

　　　　　　　A B

_____33. Larry and (me, I) have been friends for years.

　　　　　　　　　　　　　A　　　　　**B**

_____34. *Schindler's List* is one of the (most powerful, powerful) films I

have ever seen.

　　　　　　　A　　**B**

_____35. Andy's (neice, niece) began kindergarten this fall.

A B

_____36. There (are, is) only three days left to drop a course without

receiving a "W" mark on your transcripts.

A   B

_____37. (Although, In spite of the fact that) Gwen had taken a year of

chemistry in high school, she decided to take the Introduction to

Chemistry course her first semester.

A   B

_____38. I'm sorry, but I cannot (accept, except) the position you've

offered me.

A   B

_____39. Xiao considered (to transfer, transferring) to another school.

A   B

_____40. The (dog's, dogs') owners were not paying attention when the

two animals began to fight with each other.

_____41. Although our overall score was lower, we performed better than

A   B

(them, they) in several important categories.

A   B

_____42. Ilse had not (expect, expected) them to ask her what she thought

was a fair salary.

A   B

_____43. Some students are not (aware of, aware about) the services

offered by the tutorial center.

A   B

_____44. Employees were told (not to worry too much, not to get freaked

out) about the strange odors circulating through the building.

A   B

_____45. I had to work (quick, quickly) in order to leave the office in time

to make it to the party.

Part Three

For each number, choose the sentence that is correctly worded and punctuated. Write the letter indicating the correct sentence in the space provided.

_____ 46. **A.** Waiting in a long line outside the adviser's office, the adviser told the students he was about to break for lunch.

B. Waiting in a long line outside the adviser's office, the students learned that the adviser was about to break for lunch.

_____ 47. **A.** After class Jill spoke with the professor, and she complimented her on her good ideas.

B. After class Jill spoke with the professor, who complimented Jill on her good ideas.

_____ 48. **A.** Swimming, canoeing, and sailing are among the many popular activities at the lake.

B. Swimming, canoeing, and sailboats are among the many popular activities at the lake.

_____ 49. **A.** The union president said that "he now felt that a strike was unavoidable."

B. The union president said that he now felt that a strike was unavoidable.

_____ 50. **A.** As I pulled myself together, my knees shaking, my mind was in a whirl.

B. Pulling myself together, my knees shaking, my mind was in a whirl.

_____ 51. **A.** Florida, Texas, and California are among the states with the most Spanish-speaking citizens.

B. Florida Texas and California are among the states with the most Spanish-speaking citizens.

_____ 52. **A.** Sometimes making a phone call is better than an email message.

B. Sometimes making a phone call is better than sending an email message.

_____ 53. **A.** My daughter's regular pediatrican, Dr. Bruce, was out of town, so we saw Dr. Janacek instead.

B. My daughter's regular pediatrician Dr. Bruce was out of town, so we saw Dr. Janacek instead.

_____ 54. **A.** The season begun on a positive note with the Flyers winning their first three games.

        B. The season began on a positive note with the Flyers winning their first three games.

_____ 55. **A.** Here are some tips on saving money on groceries. For example: Make sure you have a full stomach when you shop, buy dry goods in large quantities, clip coupons.

        B. Here are some tips on saving money on groceries: Make sure you have a full stomach when you shop, buy dry goods in large quantities, clip coupons.

_____ 56. **A.** Is it worse to be unemployed or to hate your job?

        B. Is it worse being unemployed or to hate your job?

_____ 57. **A.** Don't try to do all your studying the night before an exam; set aside an hour or two each evening for several days in advance.

        B. Don't try to do all your studying the night before an exam, set aside an hour or two each evening for several days in advance.

_____ 58. **A.** When I read the article Rents Too High for Many to Pay, I understood exactly what the writer was talking about.

        B. When I read the article "Rents Too High for Many to Pay," I understood exactly what the writer was talking about.

_____ 59. **A.** Physics, even more so than most other areas of science, requires very strong math skills.

        B. Physics even more so than most other areas of science, requires very strong math skills.

_____ 60. **A.** Learning to swim a long distance in a pool is not that hard, the difficult thing is keeping yourself afloat for hours in the open ocean.

        B. Learning to swim a long distance in a pool is not that hard. The difficult thing is keeping yourself afloat for hours in the open ocean.

_____ 61. **A.** Speaking to shareholders, the company president said, "it now appears likely that we will show a loss for the second straight year."

        B. Speaking to shareholders, the company president said, "It now appears likely that we will show a loss for the second straight year."

_____ 62. **A.** Working as a schoolteacher can be both difficult and rewarding.

B. Working as a schoolteacher can be both difficult and it can bring rewards.

_____ 63. **A.** Before I woke up, I had been dreaming about being alone on a beach in Florida.

B. I had been dreaming about being alone on a beach in Florida before I woke up.

_____ 64. **A.** Since Keith started going to bed earlier, his concentration in class has been much better.

B. Since Keith started going to bed earlier; his concentration in class has been much better.

_____ 65. **A.** By the time her boss finally had time to talk with her Kristin's anger had cooled off.

B. By the time her boss finally had time to talk with her, Kristin's anger had cooled off.

Diagnostic Test–D: Answer Key

1. A	18. B	35. B	52. B
2. B	19. B	36. A	53. A
3. B	20. C	37. A	54. B
4. B	21. A	38. A	55. B
5. A	22. B	39. B	56. A
6. C	23. A	40. B	57. A
7. B	24. A	41. B	58. B
8. A	25. A	42. B	59. A
9. B	26. A	43. A	60. B
10. A	27. A	44. A	61. B
11. A	28. A	45. B	62. A
12. B	29. A	46. B	63. A
13. B	30. B	47. B	64. A
14. A	31. A	48. A	65. B
15. B	32. B	49. B	
16. B	33. B	50. A	
17. A	34. A	51. A	

Diagnostic Test–D

Identification of Problem Areas

The following table will help you to identify your students' strengths and weaknesses in grammar, sentence structure, punctuation, and spelling skills. Use the table to match chapter content in *Real Essays* with individual items from the diagnostic test.

Chapter in Real Essays		*Test Items*
23	Fragments	2, 19, 22, 27
24	Run-ons	9, 17, 21, 23, 57, 60
25	Problems with subject–verb agreement	3, 28, 36
26	Verb problems	1, 13, 42, 54
27	Pronouns	7, 15, 33, 41, 47
28	Adjectives and adverbs	34, 45
29	Misplaced and dangling modifiers	46, 50, 63
30	Coordination and subordination	21, 23, 27, 64
31	Parallelism	8, 48, 52, 56, 62
33	ESL	4, 10, 31, 39, 43
34	Word choice	37, 44
35	Commonly confused words	25, 30, 38
36	Spelling	5, 26, 29, 35
37	Commas	14, 24, 51, 53, 59, 65
38	Apostrophes	11, 18, 32, 40
39	Quotation marks	49, 58
40	Other punctuation	16, 19, 22, 55, 57, 64
41	Capitalization	12, 61

Review Tests for Editing Chapters
(*Chapters 22–41*)

Chapter 22: The Basic Sentence

Chapter Review Test

For each of the following sentences, identify the part of the sentence that is underlined. For verbs, distinguish between action verbs, linking verbs, and helping verbs. Write your answers in the space provided.

EXAMPLE

prepositional phrase   After graduating from high school, I needed to think seriously about what kind of career I wanted to pursue.

1. _____ My guidance counselor said that when thinking about a career, I should think about what kinds of things I enjoy doing.

2. _____ My favorite hobby is taking things apart and putting them back together.

3. _____ Mostly, I like to take apart electrical appliances.

4. _____ When I was younger, I secretly took apart my mother's clock radio.

5. _____ I didn't think that she would ever know what I had done.

6. _____ The next morning, the alarm clock did not go off.

7. _____ My mother realized what had happened to her radio, but she didn't get angry with me.

8. _____ Instead, she encouraged me to experiment with old appliances from the junkyard.

9. _____ I was unable to see how I could turn my hobby into a career until I asked my mother for advice.

10. _____ She said that of course she knew the perfect job for me—being an electrician—and, as usual, she is right.

Chapter 23: Fragments

Chapter Review Test 1

Circle the fragments in the paragraph, and then edit the paragraph so that there are no fragments.

Charcoal was invented by Henry Ford. The man who also manufactured the first cars. Ford invented a way to convert the wood scraps left over from car manufacturing into charcoal. During the 1920s. His friend, Thomas Edison, designed the factory. That manufactured the pillow-shaped briquets. In 1922, according to the Kingsford Products Company in Oakland, California. Ford turned over the charcoal operation to his relative, E. G. Kingsford. To relieve himself of some responsibilities. Until the 1950s, Kingsford charcoal couldn't be bought just anywhere. Only at Ford dealerships.

Chapter 23: Fragments

Chapter Review Test 2

Read the application letter that follows. Circle the fragments, and then edit the letter so that there are no fragments.

Dear Ms. Brown:

Please consider me as a candidate for the part-time position of administrative assistant in the marketing department. After reading your advertisement in *The San Antonion Daily*. I feel confident that I could make a valuable contribution to the company.

I am a student at San Antonio College. Pursuing a degree in business administration. I have completed courses in principles of marketing, introduction to business, managerial finance, and others that give me the skills to qualify for the administrative assistant position. My cumulative grade point average is 3.5.

I also have office and retail experience. Having held positions as secretary to the direct mail manager at Latimer Gifts, sales clerk at the Gap, and sales clerk at Payless ShoeSource. Where I was named "Employee of the Month" in September of 1996. These positions have given me an understanding of customer needs, customer service, and direct mail marketing. I believe I can apply in your company what I've learned from previous experiences. While continuing to take courses toward my degree.

I have enclosed my résumé. It provides complete information on my education and experience. To help in your selection. I have also enclosed a list of references. On a separate sheet of paper. Also a letter of recommendation. Thank you for your consideration. I will look forward to speaking with you.

Sincerely,

Marcia Perez

Chapter 24: Run-Ons

Chapter Review Test 1

Check each sentence for run-on sentences (comma splices and fused sentences). In the space to the left, write "CS" for a comma splice, "F" for a fused sentence, or "C" for correct. Then edit each sentence by adding words and/or punctuation. Do not use the same method of correction in every sentence.

_____ 1. Living with my parents used to be a drag, however, living on my own can be pretty neat.

_____ 2. Living with my parents was difficult at times, it was especially difficult once I got out of the military.

_____ 3. Dad had his rules for instance we couldn't receive any phone calls after 9:00 P.M. and had to be in before 10:00 P.M.

_____ 4. Likewise, Mom had her rules making my bed and cleaning my room before breakfast every morning was my least favorite rule.

_____ 5. And, of course, there were always the chores, I had to mow the yard, clean the bathroom, and clean my closet.

_____ 6. Now my life is a breeze, I don't have any rules to go by but my own.

_____ 7. I'm not on the phone as often as I was at home if I want to call after 9:00 P.M., I can.

_____ 8. I don't have to be home at a certain time I don't usually, for example, get home from work before 11:00 P.M.

_____ 9. Although I still have chores, they don't seem as bad since I make them up.

_____ 10. As a result, I think both living situations had their good points I still prefer living on my own.

Chapter 24: Run-Ons

Chapter Review Test 2

Identify the run-ons in the paragraph, and then edit the paragraph so that there are no run-ons.

(1) College admissions officers in large colleges and universities receive thousands of applications every year, many of the applications for fall don't come in until April or May. (2) These dates are well within the deadline there is a good reason to apply earlier. (3) In order for students to be considered for financial aid or scholarship, applications need to be received early in the calendar year. (4) Many transfer students don't realize this they wait too long and can't get money they might have been qualified to receive. (5) Early in the year a student might be awarded a grant later that same student might receive a loan. (6) The difference between the two is significant, the grant is given with no strings attached, the loan must be repaid later.

Chapter 25: Subject-Verb Agreement

Chapter Review Test 1

Read the following sentences carefully for subject–verb agreement problems. If you find a problem, write the correct form of the verb in the space provided. Mark any correct sentences with a "C."

_____ 1. The United States, land of the free, are rapidly becoming the land of the fat.

_____ 2. Therefore, everyone seem concerned with appearances.

_____ 3. Everywhere you look, people of all ages exercises and watch what they eat.

_____ 4. In my P.E. class, not one of the students like the way he or she looks.

_____ 5. Neither the students nor the teacher has any big weight problem.

_____ 6. There are, believe it or not, one student who weighs only 90 pounds.

_____ 7. However, each of the members of my exercise group want to lose 20 pounds.

_____ 8. Losing those extra pounds are not enough.

_____ 9. Men and women, no matter what their ages, need to concern themselves with staying healthy.

_____ 10. A man or woman who wants to become healthy need to exercise and to plan meals carefully.

_____ 11. My teacher says that everyone in the class have excess body fat that we need to eliminate, even the skinny person.

_____ 12. Aerobic exercise and weight training provide health benefits we need.

_____ 13. Walking, riding a bike, or jogging help improve the cardiovascular system.

_____ 14. Using weights, like ankle weights or the weight machines, build strength and energy.

_____ 15. Some of my classmates like to exercise first thing in the morning because there is no jobs or school responsibilities to distract them.

_____ 16. Working out in the afternoon, my favorite time for exercise, increase a person's energy level so he or she can finish the work or school day.

_____ 17. Nighttime exercisers has the advantages of more flexible joints, stronger muscles, and more lung capacity.

_____ 18. However, too much exercise before bedtime keep people awake.

_____ 19. How does most people get started?

_____ 20. Everyone have to plan a program that fits into the day's schedule and that allows for good exercise and appropriate rest.

Chapter 25: Subject-Verb Agreement

Chapter Review Test 2

Read the following paragraph for subject-verb agreement problems. If you find an error, write the correct verb in the proper space by the corresponding number at the bottom of the page. If the sentence is correct, write C by its corresponding number.

(1) Why do the United States, a country of freedoms, need a rating system for movies? (2) First, the rating system for all major theatrical releases are based on the contents of the movie. (3) There is major differences between R-rated movies and PG-rated movies in today's theaters. (4) An R-rated movie usually have an unbelievable amount of sex and gruesome violence; however, PG-rated movies contain very little, if any, sex or violence. (5) Furthermore, the rating system also issues warnings to the public. (6) For instance, anyone under the age of 17 need a parent along to go to an R-rated movie. (7) A PG-rated movie don't have an age limit, so anyone can see the movie. (8) Also, harsher plots appear in R-rated movies since they aim at an adult audience. (9) Thus, anyone going to an R-rated movie should not be surprised by a graphic look at the grim side of human events. (10) On the other hand, most PG-rated movies provides the audiences with more of a family-value type of thinking. (11) PG-rated movies, the majority of the time, provides more wholesome topics for the viewers. (12) Finally, knowing the distinctions between the ratings makes selecting the right movie easier.

1. _____   5. _____   9. _____

2. _____   6. _____   10. _____

3. _____   7. _____   11. _____

4. _____   8. _____   12. _____

Chapter 26: Verb Problems

Chapter Review Test 1

Write the correct form of the verb in parentheses in the space under each sentence.

1. In 1956, Handler and her husband (start) a tiny toy company called Mattel.

   _____

2. In the late 1950s and early 1960s, they (make) baby dolls.

   _____

3. Handler (raise) the idea of a doll that looked older and more realistic, but no one (think) it was a good idea.

   _____

4. Just before she came home from a trip to Europe, Handler (see) a teenaged doll.

   _____

5. She (demand) that Mattel make such a doll.

   _____

6. They (do), and the doll (become) Barbie, named after Handler's daughter.

   _____

7. Barbie (be) the world's most popular doll, and the Mattel toy company (grow) fast.

   _____

8. Today, Barbies (sell) at the rate of two per second.

   _____

9. In 1993, sales (exceed) $1 billion.

   _____

10. Today, the Handler family (live) in Denver, Colorado.

   _____

Chapter 26: Verb Problems

Chapter Review Test 2

Read the following paragraphs for errors in verb tense. If you find an error, write the correct form in the proper space by the corresponding number below the paragraphs. If the sentence is correct, write "C" by its corresponding number.

(1) Franklin Delano Roosevelt was the thirty-second president of the United States. (2) Until he was in his early thirties, he was very active and athletic. (3) He sail, ride horses, and play all kinds of sports. He perceived himself as an athlete. (4) However, as a young man, he contracts polio, and for the rest of his life could barely walk. (5) When he does walk, it is with great difficulty and only with the aid of steel crutches. (6) He did not let polio get in his way. (7) Instead, he hold public office. (8) First he become governor of New York, and then he serve three full terms as president. (9) During his terms in office, he has started hundreds of new social and economic programs, work to bring about racial equality, and has guided the country through World War II.

(10) People say that if television had exist at that time, Roosevelt would never have became president. (11) They speculate that the American people would not have elected a man in a wheelchair to the highest office in the land. (12) In the 1930s and 1940s, radio is the favorite mass medium. (13) Roosevelt was a powerful speaker, with a confident and vital voice. (14) That were the image that most people had of Roosevelt. (15) Newspapers publish photographs that showed only Roosevelt seated. (16) The average person did not think of Roosevelt as disabled. (17) Roosevelt's will and success prove that a physical disability need not hold one back from great accomplishments.

1. _____

2. _____

3. _____

4. _____

5. _____

6. _____

7. _____

8. _____

9. _____

10. _____

11. _____

12. _____

13. _____

14. _____

15. _____

16. _____

17. _____

Chapter 27: Pronouns

Chapter Review Test

The following sentences include one pronoun problem each. Circle the problem and correct it. In some cases it may be necessary to revise the entire sentence.

1. The University Finance Committee put off their decision on whether to raise tuition next year.

2. Considering the costs of tuition, room, board, and books, Joel is no longer sure that he can afford it.

3. The cost of textbooks, it has really increased a lot in recent years.

4. The woman in the financial-aid office said they don't know how much money will be available next year.

5. Can't the government find some way so that they will have more money left over for education?

6. The professor, who Joel had spoken to only once before, was glad that he had come to see her in her office.

7. Anyone who thinks that you can work full-time and take a full load of classes also needs to be prepared to go without much sleep.

8. Students study many different subjects, but they don't all interest them.

9. Ellen likes biology more than me.

10. Me and her both like business administration because it's more closely related to our career plans.

Chapter 28: Adjectives and Adverbs

Chapter Review Test

Circle the correct adjective or adverb in the sentences below.

1. This summer, in an (unusual, unusually) burst of energy, we visited three great American cities: Seattle, St. Louis, and Washington, D.C.

2. Although I enjoyed all three, I enjoyed Seattle (more, the most).

3. (Probable, Probably) the reason for my fascination with Seattle is that I had never been to the West Coast.

4. We were prepared for rainy days and cool evenings, but the weather we found was (more good, better, best) than we expected.

5. The sweater I took for cold nights kept me (comfortable, comfortably) in the daytime, and my umbrella never left my suitcase.

6. We began our (excited, exciting) excursion Saturday morning by riding the monorail to Seattle Center, the site of the 1962 World's Fair.

7. From the 520-foot observation deck of the Space Needle, we could see every area of Seattle (easily, easy) and plan our day's sightseeing.

8. Returning to downtown, we toured the Pike Place Market, the oldest (continual, continually) operating farmers' market in the United States.

9. Then we started the steep descent to the Waterfront for a (good, well) lunch of fresh grilled fish.

10. That afternoon found us in Pioneer Square for a tour of Underground Seattle, where we learned how disagreements among early town settlers and the town's (unique, uniquely) plumbing problems led to streets being built 10 feet above original streets.

11. Although the day had been (real, really) fun, we were exhausted and ready for a quick dinner and bed.

12. However, our hotel staff insisted our trip wouldn't be complete without a dinner on Redondo Beach, so out we headed for a (relaxed, relaxing) meal with a beautiful view of the water.

13. On Sunday afternoon, we traveled to Snoqualmie Falls, which at 270 feet is 100 feet (higher, more high) than Niagara Falls.

14. The scenery was as (spectacular, spectacularly) breathtaking as it was in the TV show *Twin Peaks,* which was filmed there.

15. Then we drove to Mercer Island for Mother's Day dinner with friends and a (rough, roughly) boat ride around Lake Washington.

16. On Monday morning, we toured the Museum of Flight, housed in the Boeing Company's original home—a red barn—and saw a (large, larger) collection of fifty-six planes, including Air Force One.

17. We spent our last afternoon enjoying the sights, sounds, and cuisine of Chinatown with its (dramatic, dramatically) and colorful pagoda donated by the City of Taipei.

18. For our last evening in town, we took a harbor cruise to Blake Island's Tillicum Village for a great smoked salmon dinner, beautiful scenery, and a (most unique, unique) program illustrating the dances and legends of Northwest Coast Indians.

19. The (worse, worst) part of the trip was having to leave the impressive view of Mount Rainier that we had from our hotel room.

20. Flying out Tuesday morning, we decided we had managed our time (good, well) and had seen more of Seattle than we had imagined possible.

Chapter 29: Misplaced and Dangling Modifiers

Chapter Review Test

Rewrite each sentence to eliminate problems with misplaced and dangling modifiers. In some cases, it may be necessary to add additional words.

1. Arriving at the bookstore, the two books Seung-Yeun needed for her writing class were nowhere to be found.

2. She searched through several stacks and shelves becoming increasingly irritated.

3. At the front desk, Seung-Yeun told the names of the books to the bookstore manager she was unable to find.

4. The manager said that he had almost ordered one hundred additional copies and that they would arrive within a few days.

5. The textbooks still had not been delivered to the bookstore manager's surprise a week later.

6. Anxious not to fall behind in her work, Seung-Yeun's instructor gave her photocopied materials from the textbooks.

7. Difficult to read because the print was too dark, Seung-Yeun finally gave up on the photocopied section and borrowed a classmate's textbook instead.

8. The bookstore manager said the next day that the books finally had arrived, feeling bad about their delay.

9. Being a good businessman, the books were discounted 10 percent for Seung-Yeun.

10. She paid for her purchase and ran off to class with her books showing gratitude with a handshake and a smile.

Chapter 30: Coordination and Subordination

Chapter Review Test

The following paragraph has too many choppy sentences. Join at least three pairs of sentences using either coordination or subordination.

There is a building in Washington, D.C., with an interesting history. According to some stories, unknown facts about the assassination of Abraham Lincoln are hidden in one of the columns supporting the building. Lincoln's son, Robert, was secretary of war. He learned of documents that showed his father's murder was a conspiracy, not just the act of John Wilkes Booth alone. He got the documents. He was reluctant to reveal them to the country. He concealed them in a column of a building. It was under construction. Apparently Lincoln intended the documents for posterity. No one knows where the documents are, or if they really exist. Their possible existence is a part of Washington, D.C., folklore.

Chapter 31: Parallelism

Chapter Review Test

Read the following paragraph. On a separate piece of paper or on a computer, write the numbers of the sentences that aren't parallel, and then rewrite them in parallel form.

(1) Good relationships require love, respect, and communicating. (2) Avoiding arguments may seem easier than to confront the problem. (3) But over time, avoidance is as destructive to a relationship as constant disagreement is. (4) When couples don't talk to each other, they may not only avoid conflict but also losing the ability to communicate. (5) When this happens, relationships tend either to die or they stagnate. (6) Without communication, relationships can't withstand the pressures of working, taking care of household responsibilities, and parenting. (7) Couples have to talk about both their problems and solving them. (8) If they can discuss things with respect and trust, they can work out problems. (9) Without communicating, love and respect may not be enough.

Chapter 32: Sentence Variety

Chapter Review Test

Create sentence variety in the paragraphs that follow. Edit at least two sentences in each of the paragraphs. Try to use several of the techniques covered in this chapter.

Every country has its own traditions and holiday celebrations. We would expect those traditions and holidays to be very different. Many are. Some are surprisingly similar. New Year's celebrations across the world have one major similarity. The celebrants wish for good luck and wealth as they welcome in the new year.

We are familiar with the United States' traditions. Family and friends dress up and go out to a nice restaurant or club. Other people invite friends to a big party at their homes. Everyone drinks champagne, uses noisemakers, and watches the dropping ball in New York's Times Square at midnight on New Year's Eve. No one can leave the table until he or she has eaten black-eyed peas for good luck in the coming year.

Several other countries have food as a big part of the New Year's celebration. Pork is especially popular in many countries such as Brazil. Celebrants in Poland enjoy pig's feet galantine, an aspic-wrapped paté. Italians serve sausage and lentils. They represent the prosperity of a wallet full of money. The Chinese apply a fresh coat of red paint to their front doors for good luck and happiness and serve pork dumplings. The Swedish New Year begins with breakfast in bed. It consists of pork sausage on a bun with an apple. The Austrians are the most elaborate. They serve a suckling pig. They place it on a table laid out with tiny pig-shaped cookies, candy, and peppermint ice cream shaped like a four-leaf clover. They eat that for dessert.

Other food traditions are found across the world. In the Middle East, people eat pomegranate seeds to ensure fertility. The Japanese serve a dish called *mochi*. *Mochi* is pounded rice cakes. A celebration in Norway would include rice pudding prepared with one whole almond. Tradition says that whoever finds the almond is guaranteed wealth in the new year.

Sicilians eat lasagna. Partygoers in Spain eat twelve grapes at midnight. They eat one at each strike of the clock. The grapes stand for good luck for each month. The Greeks bake a special New Year's bread. It contains a buried coin. The first slice is for the Christ child. The second slice is for the head of the household. Everyone watches when the third slice is cut. If it exposes the coin, it means that an early spring is predicted.

Food is not part of the tradition in England and Scotland. The first person over the threshold after midnight in those two countries is supposed to be a male. The man brings a gift of a piece of coal for the fire. The coal will bring warmth to the house in the new year. The man must enter through the front door and leave through the back door for good luck. People in Wales open the front door to let in the new year, and open and close the back door to let out any bad luck from the old year. The traditions may be different. They all rely on superstitions for good luck.

Chapter 33: ESL Concerns

Chapter Review Test

Edit the following sentences to make the nouns and articles correct.

1. When I moved to Florida, I wanted to go to beach.

2. I never lived near a water and wanted to walk on the sands.

3. I took big umbrella, dog, and Frisbee with me.

4. When waves washed up on shore, I found seashell and clam.

5. For lunch, I bought hot dog and cola from restaurant.

Find and correct any problems with verbs in the sentences below.

6. Coming to this country was one of the most interesting challenges that I experience in my life.

7. First of all, everything is different here, so to adjust was difficult for me.

8. The opportunity for education and self-improvement will changing my life.

9. After all, I am capable to live with freedom and exposing my mind to new ideas.

10. Overall, this immigration has made me to face all my dreams and wishes.

Edit the following sentences to make sure that prepositions are used correctly.

11. If you want a job, you must first fill up an application form at the company's personnel office.

12. Don't be afraid to going for an interview because the personnel director will be very nice to you.

13. Make sure that you show the employer that you are excited on working for her company.

14. If she hires you, the employer will go to all of the duties of the job and the company's policies.

15. If you are confused in the directions, just ask questions.

For each positive statement below, write one negative statement and one question.

16. All writers experience writer's block.

    _____

    _____

17. You can start writing about a topic that you choose.

    _____

    _____

18. You can pretend to write a letter to a friend.

    _____

    _____

19. Some writers enjoy describing happy memories.

    _____

    _____

20. Other people like to imagine their lives one year from now.

    _____

    _____

Chapter 34: Word Choice

Chapter Review Test

Find and edit any examples of vague and abstract language, slang, wordy language, or clichés in the following paragraphs.

Americans seem to have a fascination with food. Whether it's cooking, eating, shopping, or talking about it, food dominates much of our time and energies. In fact, food can be both good and bad for you. However, whereas food is a life-sustaining necessity, Americans have gone overboard.

In this day and age, fast-food places dominate the highways, and it looks to me like you can't even drive two blocks without seeing a McDonald's or a Taco Bell. If Mom's too dragged out from a hard day at work, she just takes a pass through the drive-through window at the neighborhood chicken shack. In the event that Dad is rushing from here to there during his busy day, he gobbles down a sandwich and chugs down a soda as he drives to his next appointment. Even the family that has spent a leisurely day at home working in the garden or merely enjoying the relative comforts of their home will call for pizza delivery rather than take the time to prepare a nice home-cooked meal.

To the other extreme are the health fanatics. You won't catch a burger and fries sliding over their tongues. No, sir. Their refrigerators look like the produce department at the local grocery store. You won't find any red meat in their homes, but you can find a lot of that green, leafy stuff. Plus, they have an abundant supply of carrots, broccoli, zucchini, and tomatoes in addition. You might as well rename that home "Rabbit Hutch." And forget the sweets. Fruit (with perhaps a fat-free cereal bar thrown in for good measure) is what these people consider dessert. In their opinion, these people believe that vegetables and whole grains are the only way to go.

Probably somewhere in between are the ones who enjoy food but don't take it too seriously. They enjoy a good burger every now and then, but they also count calories and watch their fat intake. Mom and Dad and even the kids will pitch in and produce an evening meal fit for a queen (or king). They carefully itemize the ingredients and try to figure out if all of the food groups are properly included in the family's last meal of the day.

The fact of the matter is that with so many different kinds of eaters, food has become big business. From fancy restaurants to fast-food drive-throughs, Americans have a big choice when it comes to eating out. But even grocery stores are getting into the prepared-food picture. Their deli sections offer a lot of things. For the person who wants to pretend to have a hand in the food preparation, grocery stores have marinated meats and vegetable dishes that are ready to stick right in the oven as soon as the buyer arrives home. Whatever their tastes and styles, Americans can find what they want. Remember: We are what we eat.

Chapter 35: Commonly Confused Words

Chapter Review Test

In the following sentences, circle the correct word in parentheses.

1. The waiters are paying more attention to the television than to what (their, there, they're) supposed to be doing.

2. The lottery has bigger and more negative aspects (than, then) good ones.

3. I (preceded, proceeded) to tell my four-year-old daughter that she had both of her legs in one pants hole.

4. My hands blistered when I accidentally stuck them (to, too, two) far into the broiler.

5. Alice should not (pass, past) judgment on other people.

6. (Who's, Whose) to say that is the right solution?

7. The children would (loose, lose) the chance to meet new friends, learn leadership skills, and have some fun in their lives.

8. Where is (are, our) money going?

9. Sometimes patients think they (know, no) more than the doctors do.

10. (Weather, Whether) the doctor wants to or not, it is his responsibility to inform patients of their choices.

11. No one in the family wanted my father to go (though, through, threw) with the heart transplant.

12. Tamara was (suppose, supposed) to wash the dishes before going to the movie.

13. Jason answered all of the test questions (accept, except) those dealing with the Hopi Indians.

14. As soon as he saw the chemistry test, Jerry realized that he should (of, have) studied more.

15. If we (by, buy) season tickets to the symphony, we can get better seats for the special shows.

16. Although the patient was (conscience, conscious) when he arrived at the hospital, he soon lapsed into a coma.

17. The singer's pants were so (loose, lose) that I thought they would fall off.

18. Because she was angry, Beatriz (set, sit) the glass down so hard that it broke.

19. Moderate to brisk walking can significantly improve (your, you're) fitness level.

20. Before he invested his summer earnings, Syed wanted the (advice, advise) of his stockbroker.

Chapter 36: Spelling

Chapter Review Test

Find and correct any spelling errors in the following paragraphs.

(1) When I first met my college roommate, I was suprized at how much we had in common. (2) For instance, we were both the same hieght and had the same color hair. (3) We also had similiar body shapes. (4) In fact, we were so much alike that our goverment teacher always got us confused. (5) He finally had to seperate us in class when he acidentaly gave Todd my grade.

(6) Both being nonscholarship atheletes, we tried out for the football team. (7) However, the coach thought we weren't strong enough, so he told us to develop muscles and body mass during our freshman year and try again when we were sophomores. (8) Todd and I started a fitness program imedi-ately. (9) We worked out on the Nautilus equitment in the gym three days a week, and on weekends we rode our bicycles fourty miles. (10) Even during the horrable weather in January and Febuary, we managed to keep our train-ing schedule. (11) By the end of the spring term, we had sucessfully reached our goal wieght and proportions. (12) However, by that time, we had joined a fraternity and decided to give up sports, except for fraternity activities.

(13) Todd and I also had the same carrer goals. (14) We both were per-suing a degree in bussiness managment. (15) We immersed ourselves totaly in our studies and spent alot of time in the library. (16) We decided that the benifits of studying would definately surpass those of playing football. (17) We were proved right when the personell director of a local firm hired us as interns. (18) Who would have guessed that instead of lonelyness, I would find a lifelong friend when I moved away to school?

Chapter 37: Commas

Chapter Review Test

Add any necessary commas in the following sentences. If a sentence is correct, circle the number.

1. The one accomplishment I am most proud of is my car a 1966 Ford Mustang because I have paid for all repairs and improvements with my money.

2. When I first got my car it didn't have a very good paint job.

3. I worked extra hours didn't go to movies asked for money for my birthday and saved every dollar I received.

4. Although expensive, the paint that I selected made the car look ten years newer.

5. Soon after I got my paint job I had to put more hard-earned money into my car.

6. The transmission on the car was old so it went crazy.

7. I had no parking gear and some other gears were gone also.

8. In fact, I had only reverse neutral and one other gear.

9. I was without a car for a couple of weeks while the repair shop rebuilt my transmission but I kept saving as much money as possible during that time.

10. After the transmission was fixed I was satisfied with the car for a little while.

11. Then I decided that I wanted floor mats a new steering wheel a stereo and chrome wheels.

12. Luckily it didn't take long to save enough money for mats and a steering wheel.

13. My next goal was chrome wheels which would make my beautiful car look even better.

14. I soon discovered that the wheels would of course cost more than I had thought.

15. My dad surprised me by saying he would pay for two of the wheels for he wanted to help me out a little bit since I had worked so hard.

16. Now the car looks great runs well and is comfortable to drive.

17. You would think wouldn't you that I would be completely happy.

18. Now I want a stereo which will provide additional enjoyment to my driving time.

19. My current goal is to buy an Alpine stereo a CD changer and great speakers by Christmas.

20. Even if I miss that goal I'll know that I have a great car that I paid for myself.

Chapter 38: Apostrophes

Chapter Review Test

Read the following sentences for correct use and placement of apostrophes. Add missing apostrophes, and delete unnecessary apostrophes. Some sentences may have more than one error.

1. Because Pat cant make up his mind, he changes his plan's several times a day.

2. Fiona receives $10 from her parents if she gets all As and Bs on her grade report.

3. After we return from our months vacation, well respond to all the mail and phone messages.

4. Our cat wants it's food in a secluded area, whereas our dogs want their's in the family room.

5. No one want's to live in a vegetative state, unable to eat, walk, or communicate.

6. Therefore, members of the family should be the one's to make the critical medical decision instead of the doctors.

7. The problem is that a doctors word should not be allowed to override the familys decision regarding a loved one.

8. Because Sirkku put too many 0s on the bill, the accounting clerk wrote a check for $100,000 instead of $1,000.

9. Theres never enough time to complete all of the homework assignments in Mr. Buchanans class.

10. Bonnie will buy her shirt in the childrens department because its less expensive than one from the womens department.

Chapter 39: Quotation Marks

Chapter Review Test

Read the following sentences for correct use and placement of quotation marks. Make any necessary corrections. If a sentence is already correct, circle the number.

1. If you want to sell your house more quickly, the realtor advised, paint the interior and keep the yard mowed.

2. She also told us that location is the most important consideration when buying a home.

3. She also suggested that we read How to Sell Your Home for the Best Price, an article in last month's *Consumer Reports*.

4. Do you think we should have the carpets and drapes cleaned? my mother asked.

5. Don't bother to read Chapter Three, class, the teacher announced. You will be tested only on Chapters Two and Four.

6. One student bravely raised his hand and asked, Can we use our textbooks or notes during the test?

7. I read the chapter titled The Toxicity of Lead three times before I understood it.

8. One of my favorite albums is *Red Hot & Blue*. It is a tribute to Cole Porter by a variety of modern singers, Michelle said.

9. She explained that the album has songs by Sinead O'Connor, the Thompson Twins, Tom Waits, the Fine Young Cannibals, and Debbie Harry.

10. Perhaps we would have heard the doorbell if we had not been listening to k.d. lang singing Cole Porter's song So in Love.

Chapter 40: Other Punctuation

Chapter Review Test

Add colons, semicolons, parentheses, dashes, or hyphens to the following sentences.

1. Health issues ranging from nutrition to exercise to disease have progressively invaded our homes and our everyday lives.

2. Driving in our cars a major part of our daily schedule, we see billboards promoting items that relate to health.

3. While flying down the highway, we might hear on the radio about a two for one special at a health club or maybe a diet cola jingle.

4. Another place for such information would be on restaurant menus, where we might find sections for people with special dietary concerns low fat, low sodium, low cholesterol.

5. Nutrition including the types and amounts of food that we eat plays a big role in one way of staying healthy.

6. More nutritional foods that appeal to a large number of people salads, vegetable platters, diet drinks can now be found on most menus.

7. In addition, most every food product we buy in the grocery store has a list of nutritional facts on the outer label size and number of servings, fat content, number of calories, and amounts of carbohydrates and protein.

8. Television provides the most common source of information there we can see cooking shows that emphasize healthy cooking and paid programs for home exercise equipment.

9. Public service announcements appear on radio and television and in magazines promoting good habits and healthy lifestyles for instance, they warn against drug abuse, heavy smoking, and drinking and driving.

10. With such widespread illustrations, it is easy to conclude that America has become a health conscious nation.

Chapter 41: Capitalization

Chapter Review Test

Read the following sentences and edit for correct capitalization.

1. Vacations offer a wide variety of opportunities whether you are traveling in europe, north or south america, asia, or the united states.

2. between june and august, you can take a week-long cruise between sitka and juneau, alaska, to view humpback whales, otters, seals, and glaciers.

3. If you vacation in denali national park, you can enjoy river rafting, nature hikes, cruises among the glaciers, and minibus tours.

4. my Aunt and Uncle enjoyed their fourteen-day caribbean cruise that included visits to martinique and st. martin and lots of creole food.

5. One of my favorite vacation spots is colorado springs, where i can visit natural wonders such as seven falls and pike's peak.

6. While visiting Washington, d.c., you need to see the famous Monuments, the white house, and ford's theatre.

7. A short train ride out of boston will take you to the Church that contains the crypts of president john adams and president john quincy adams.

8. If you have children, you might consider a trip to florida for fun times at disney world, sea world, and universal studios.

9. For the person who likes to shop, mall of the americas in minneapolis provides the world's largest selection of shops under one roof, as well as restaurants, a skating rink, a huge Lego display, and an amusement park.

10. You can find great information for travel in publications such as *national geographic* and from organizations such as a local Chamber of Commerce and the American automobile association.

Chapter 22: The Basic Sentence

Answers to Chapter Review Test

1. action verb   2. helping verb   3. adjective   4. adverb   5. pronoun
6. phrase   7. coordinating conjunction   8. preposition   9. linking verb
10. noun

Chapter 23: Fragments

Answers to Chapter Review Test 1

FRAGMENTS

The man who also manufactured the first cars.

During the 1920s.

That manufactured the pillow-shaped briquets.

In 1922, according to the Kingsford Products Company in Oakland, California.

To relieve himself of some responsibilities.

Only at Ford dealerships.

POSSIBLE REVISIONS

Charcoal was invented by Henry Ford, the man who also manufactured the first cars. Ford invented a way to convert the wood scraps left over from car manufacturing into charcoal during the 1920s. His friend, Thomas Edison, designed the factory that manufactured the pillow-shaped briquets. In 1922, according to the Kingsford Products Company in Oakland, California, Ford turned over the charcoal operation to his relative, E. G. Kingsford in order to relieve himself of some responsibilities. Until the 1950s, Kingsford charcoal couldn't be bought just anywhere, only at Ford dealerships.

Chapter 23: Fragments

Answers to Chapter Review Test 2

FRAGMENTS

After reading your advertisement in *The San Antonion Daily.*

Pursuing a degree in business administration.

Having held positions as secretary to the direct mail manager at Latimer Gifts, sales clerk at the Gap, and sales clerk at Payless ShoeSource.

Where I was named "Employee of the Month" in September of 1996.

While continuing to take courses toward my degree.

To help in your selection.

On a separate sheet of paper.

Also a letter of recommendation.

POSSIBLE REVISIONS

Dear Ms. Brown:

Please consider me as a candidate for the part-time position of administrative assistant in the marketing department. After reading your advertisement in *The San Antonion Daily,* I feel confident that I could make a valuable contribution to the company.

I am a student at San Antonio College pursuing a degree in business administration. I have completed courses in principles of marketing, introduction to business, managerial finance, and others that give me the skills to qualify for the administrative assistant position. My cumulative grade point average is 3.5.

I also have office and retail experience, having held positions as secretary to the direct mail manager at Latimer Gifts, sales clerk at the Gap, and sales clerk at Payless ShoeSource, where I was named "Employee of the Month" in September of 1996. These positions have given me an understanding of customer needs, customer service, and direct mail marketing. I believe I can apply in your company what I've learned from previous experiences while continuing to take courses toward my degree.

I have enclosed my résumé. It provides complete information on my education and experience. To help in your selection, I have also enclosed a list of references on a separate sheet of paper and a letter of recommendation. Thank you for your consideration. I will look forward to speaking with you.

Sincerely,

Marcia Perez

Chapter 24: Run-Ons

Answers to Chapter Review Test 1

1. CS   2. CS   3. F   4. F   5. CS   6. CS   7. F   8. F   9. C   10. F

POSSIBLE REVISIONS

1. Living with my parents used to be a drag; however, living on my own can be pretty neat.

2. Living with my parents was difficult at times, but it was especially difficult once I got out of the military.

3. Dad had his rules; for instance, we couldn't receive any phone calls after 9:00 P.M. and had to be in before 10:00 P.M.

4. Likewise, Mom had her rules. Making my bed and cleaning my room before breakfast every morning was my least favorite rule.

5. And, of course, there were always the chores; I had to mow the yard, clean the bathroom, and clean my closet.

6. Now my life is a breeze because I don't have any rules to go by but my own.

7. I'm not on the phone as often as I was at home, and if I want to call after 9:00 P.M., I can.

8. I don't have to be home at a certain time. I don't usually, for example, get home from work before 11:00 P.M.

9. Correct

10. As a result, I think both living situations had their good points, but I still prefer living on my own.

Chapter 24: Run-Ons

Answers to Chapter Review Test 2

RUN-ONS

Sentences 1, 2, 4, 5, and 6

POSSIBLE REVISIONS

College admissions officers in large colleges and universities receive thousands of applications every year. Many of the applications for fall don't come in until April or May. While these dates are well within the deadline, there is a good reason to apply earlier. In order for students to be considered for financial aid or scholarship, applications need to be received early in the calendar year. Many transfer students don't realize this. They wait too long and can't get money they might have been qualified to receive. Early in the year a student might be awarded a grant, but later that same student might receive a loan. The difference between the two is significant: The grant is given with no strings attached, but the loan must be repaid later.

Chapter 25: Subject-Verb Agreement

Answers to Chapter Review Test 1

1. is 2. seems 3. exercise 4. likes 5. C 6. is 7. wants 8. is 9. C
10. needs 11. has 12. C 13. helps 14. builds 15. are 16. increases
17. have 18. keeps 19. do 20. has

Chapter 25: Subject-Verb Agreement

Answers to Chapter Review Test 2

1. does 2. is 3. are 4. has 5. C 6. needs 7. doesn't 8. C 9. C
10. provide 11. provide 12. C

Chapter 26: Verb Problems

Answers to Chapter Review Test 1

1. started 2. made 3. raised; thought 4. saw 5. demanded 6. did;
became 7. was; grew 8. sell 9. exceeded 10. lives

Chapter 26: Verb Problems

Answers to Chapter Review Test 2

1. Correct 2. Correct 3. sailed; rode; played (first sentence); second sentence
is correct 4. contracted 5. did walk; was 6. Correct 7. held 8. became;
served 9. started; worked; guided 10. had existed; have become 11. Correct
12. was 13. Correct 14. was 15. published 16. Correct 17. Correct

Chapter 27: Pronouns

Answers to Chapter Review Test

1. The University Finance Committee put off its decision on whether to raise tuition next year.

2. Considering the costs of tuition, room, board, and books, Joel is no longer sure that he can afford to attend college.

3. The cost of textbooks has really increased a lot in recent years.

4. The woman in the financial-aid office said <u>she doesn't</u> know how much money will be available next year.

5. Can't the government find some way so that <u>it</u> will have more money left over for education?

6. The professor, <u>whom</u> Joel had spoken to only once before, was glad that he had come to see her in her office.

7. Anyone who thinks that <u>he or she</u> can work full-time and take a full load of classes also needs to be prepared to go without much sleep.

8. Students study many different subjects, but <u>not all of the subjects</u> interest them.

9. Ellen likes biology more than <u>I do</u>.

10. <u>She and I</u> both like business administration because it's more closely related to our career plans.

Chapter 28: Adjectives and Adverbs

Answers to Chapter Review Test

1. unusual 2. the most 3. Probably 4. better 5. comfortable 6. exciting 7. easily 8. continually 9. good 10. unique 11. really 12. relaxing 13. higher 14. spectacularly 15. rough 16. large 17. dramatic 18. unique 19. worst 20. well

Chapter 29: Misplaced and Dangling Modifiers

POSSIBLE REVISIONS

1. When Seung-Yeun arrived at the bookstore, the two books she needed for her writing class were nowhere to be found.

2. Becoming increasingly irritated, she searched through several stacks and shelves.

3. At the front desk, Seung-Yeun told the bookstore manager the names of the books she was unable to find.

4. The manager said that he had ordered almost one hundred additional copies and that they would arrive within a few days.

5. To the bookstore manager's surprise, the textbooks still had not been delivered a week later.

6. Anxious not to fall behind in her work, Seung-Yeun received from her instructor photocopied materials from the textbooks.

7.   Finding the photocopied section difficult to read because the print was too dark, Seung-Yeun finally gave up on it and borrowed a classmate's textbook instead.

8.   Feeling bad about their delay, the bookstore manager said the next day that the books finally had arrived.

9.   Being a good businessman, the bookstore manager discounted the books 10 percent for Seung-Yeun.

10. Showing gratitude with a handshake and a smile, she paid for her purchase and ran off to class with her books.

Chapter 30: Coordination and Subordination

POSSIBLE REVISIONS

There is a building in Washington, D.C., with an interesting history. According to some stories, unknown facts about the assassination of Abraham Lincoln are hidden in one of the columns supporting the building. Lincoln's son Robert was secretary of war when he learned of documents that showed his father's murder was a conspiracy, not just the act of John Wilkes Booth alone. He got the documents, but he was reluctant to reveal them to the country. Instead, he concealed them in a column of a building while it was under construction. Apparently Lincoln intended the documents for posterity, but no one knows where the documents are, or if they really exist. Their possible existence is a part of Washington, D.C., folklore.

Chapter 31: Parallelism

Answers to Chapter Review Test

Sentences that are not parallel: 1, 2, 3, 4, 5, 7, 9

POSSIBLE REVISIONS

(1) Good relationships require love, respect, and communication. (2) Avoiding arguments may seem easier than confronting the problem. (3) But over time, avoidance is as destructive to a relationship as constant disagreement. (4) When couples don't talk to each other, they may not only avoid conflict but also lose the ability to communicate. (5) When this happens, relationships tend either to die or to stagnate. (6) Without communication, relationships can't withstand the pressures of working, taking care of household responsibilities, and parenting. (7) Couples have to talk about both their problems and their solutions. (8) If they can discuss things with respect and trust, they can work out problems. (9) Without communication, love and respect may not be enough.

Chapter 32: Sentence Variety

POSSIBLE REVISIONS

Every country has its own traditions and holiday celebrations, which we would expect to be very different. Many are. Surprisingly, some are similar. Across the world, New Year's celebrations have one major similarity: The celebrants wish for good luck and wealth as they welcome in the new year.

We are familiar with the United States' traditions. Some families and friends dress up and go out to a nice restaurant or club, while other people invite friends to a big party at their homes. Drinking champagne, using noise-makers, and watching the dropping ball in New York's Times Square at midnight are standard on New Year's Eve. No one can leave the table until he or she has eaten black-eyed peas for good luck in the coming year.

Several other countries have food as a big part of the New Year's celebration. Pork is especially popular in countries such as Brazil. Celebrants in Poland enjoy pig's feet galantine, an aspic-wrapped paté. Italians serve sausage and lentils, which represent the prosperity of a wallet full of money. The Chinese, who apply a fresh coat of red paint to their front doors for good luck and happiness, serve pork dumplings. The Swedish New Year begins with breakfast in bed, consisting of pork sausage on a bun with an apple. The Austrians, the most elaborate celebrants, serve a suckling pig placed on a table laid out with tiny pig-shaped cookies, candy, and peppermint ice cream shaped like a four-leaf clover, which they eat for dessert.

Other food traditions are found across the world. In the Middle East, people eat pomegranate seeds to ensure fertility. The Japanese serve a dish called *mochi*, which is pounded rice cakes. A celebration in Norway would include rice pudding prepared with one whole almond. Finding the almond, tradition says, guarantees wealth in the new year.

Sicilians eat lasagna. Eating one grape at each strike of the clock, party-goers in Spain eat twelve grapes at midnight, one for good luck for each month. The Greeks bake a special New Year's bread containing a buried coin. The first slice is for the Christ child. The second slice is for the head of the household. Everyone watches when the third slice is cut, and if it exposes the coin, it means that an early spring is predicted.

Food is not part of the tradition in England and Scotland. In those two countries, the first person over the threshold after midnight is supposed to be a male. The man, who must enter through the front door and leave through the back door for good luck, brings a gift of a piece of coal for the fire. The coal will bring warmth to the house in the new year. Opening the front door to let in the new year, and opening and closing the back door to let out any bad luck from the old year, are customs of Welsh tradition. The traditions, though different, all rely on superstitions for good luck.

Chapter 33: ESL Concerns

Answers to Chapter Review Test

1. When I moved to Florida, I wanted to go to <u>the</u> beach.

2. I never lived near water and wanted to walk on the sands.

3. I took <u>a</u> big umbrella, <u>a</u> dog, and <u>a</u> Frisbee with me.

4. When waves washed up on <u>the</u> shore, I found <u>a</u> seashell and <u>a</u> clam.

5. For lunch, I bought <u>a</u> hot dog and <u>a</u> cola from <u>the</u> restaurant.

6. Coming to this country was one of the most interesting challenges that I <u>had experienced</u> in my life.

7. First of all, everything <u>was</u> different here, so <u>adjusting</u> was difficult for me.

8. The opportunity for education and self-improvement will <u>change</u> my life.

9. After all, I am capable <u>of living</u> with freedom and exposing my mind to new ideas.

10. Overall, this immigration has made me face all my dreams and wishes.

11. If you want a job, you must first fill <u>out</u> an application form at the company's personnel office.

12. Don't be afraid <u>of</u> going for an interview because the personnel director will be very nice to you.

13. Make sure that you show the employer that you are excited <u>to work</u> for her company.

14. If she hires you, the employer will go <u>through</u> all of the duties of the job and the company's policies.

15. If you are confused <u>by</u> the directions, just ask questions.

16. Not all writers experience writer's block.
    Do all writers experience writer's block?

17. You can't start writing about a topic that you choose.
    Can you start writing about a topic that you choose?

18. You can't pretend to write a letter to a friend.
    Can you pretend to write a letter to a friend?

19. Some writers do not enjoy describing happy memories.
    Do some writers enjoy describing happy memories?

20. Other people do not like to imagine their lives one year from now.
    Do other people like to imagine their lives one year from now?

Chapter 34: Word Choice

POSSIBLE REVISIONS

Americans seem to have a fascination with food. Whether it's cooking, eating, shopping, or talking about it, food dominates much of our time and energies. In fact, food can be both good and bad for you. <u>Whereas</u> food is a life-sustaining necessity, Americans have <u>become quite obsessed</u>.

<u>Today</u>, fast-food places dominate the highways, and it <u>seems as if</u> you can't even drive two blocks without seeing a McDonald's or a Taco Bell. If Mom's too <u>exhausted</u> from a hard day at work, she just <u>stops at</u> the drive-through window at the neighborhood chicken shack. <u>If</u> Dad is rushing <u>all over</u> during his busy day, he gobbles down a sandwich and <u>gulps</u> a soda as he drives to his next appointment. Even the family that has spent a leisurely day working in the garden or enjoying the comforts of their home will call for pizza delivery rather than take the time to prepare a nice home-cooked meal.

To the other extreme are the health fanatics. You won't <u>see them eating hamburgers and french fries</u>. Their refrigerators look like the produce department at the local grocery store. You won't find any red meat in their homes, but you can find a lot of <u>leafy greens</u>. <u>They also</u> have an abundant supply of carrots, broccoli, zucchini, and tomatoes. You might as well rename that home "Rabbit Hutch." And forget the sweets. Fruit (with perhaps a fat-free cereal bar thrown in for good measure) is what these people consider dessert. In their opinion, vegetables and whole grains <u>are the staples of a healthy diet</u>.

Probably somewhere in between are the ones who enjoy food but don't <u>become obsessive about it</u>. They enjoy a good burger every now and then, but they also count calories and watch their fat intake. Mom and Dad and even the kids will <u>help out</u> and produce a <u>delicious</u> evening meal. They carefully itemize the ingredients and <u>make sure that</u> all of the food groups are properly included in the <u>evening meal</u>.

With so many different kinds of eaters, food has become big business. From fancy restaurants to fast-food drive-throughs, Americans have a <u>wide variety of choices</u> when it comes to eating out. But even grocery stores are <u>stocking some prepared foods</u>. Their deli sections offer <u>fried chicken, salads, cooked vegetables, and desserts</u>. For the person who wants to pretend to <u>prepare the meals</u>, grocery stores have marinated meats and vegetable dishes that are ready to stick right in the oven as soon as the buyer arrives home. Whatever their tastes and styles, Americans can find what they want.

Chapter 35: Commonly Confused Words

Answers to Chapter Review Test

1. they're 2. than 3. proceeded 4. too 5. pass 6. Who's 7. lose 8. our
9. know 10. Whether 11. through 12. supposed 13. except 14. have
15. buy 16. conscious 17. loose 18. set 19. your 20. advice

Chapter 36: Spelling

Answers to Chapter Review Test

1. surprised 2. height 3. similar 4. government 5. separate; accidentally 6. athletes 7. Correct 8. immediately 9. equipment; forty 10. horrible; February 11. successfully; weight 12. Correct 13. career 14. pursuing; business; management 15. totally; a lot 16. benefits; definitely 17. personnel 18. loneliness

Chapter 37: Commas

Answers to Chapter Review Test

1. The one accomplishment I am most proud of is my car, a 1966 Ford Mustang, because I have paid for all repairs and improvements with my money.

2. When I first got my car, it didn't have a very good paint job.

3. I worked extra hours, didn't go to movies, asked for money for my birthday, and saved every dollar I received.

4. Correct.

5. Soon after I got my paint job, I had to put more hard-earned money into my car.

6. The transmission on the car was old, so it went crazy.

7. I had no parking gear, and some other gears were gone also.

8. In fact, I had only reverse, neutral, and one other gear.

9. I was without a car for a couple of weeks while the repair shop rebuilt my transmission, but I kept saving as much money as possible during that time.

10. After the transmission was fixed, I was satisfied with the car for a little while.

11. Then I decided that I wanted floor mats, a new steering wheel, a stereo, and chrome wheels.

12. Luckily, it didn't take long to save money for mats and a steering wheel.

13. My next goal was chrome wheels, which would make my beautiful car look even better.

14. I soon discovered that the wheels would, of course, cost more than I had thought.

15. My dad surprised me by saying he would pay for two of the wheels, for he wanted to help me out a little bit since I had worked so hard.

16. Now the car looks great, runs well, and is comfortable to drive.

17. You would think, wouldn't you, that I would be completely happy.

18. Now I want a stereo, which will provide additional enjoyment to my driving time.

19. My current goal is to buy an Alpine stereo, a CD changer, and great speakers by Christmas.

20. Even if I miss that goal, I'll know that I have a great car that I paid for myself.

Chapter 38: Apostrophes

Answers to Chapter Review Test

1. Because Pat <u>can't</u> make up his mind, he changes his <u>plans</u> several times a day.

2. Fiona receives $10 from her parents if she gets all <u>A's</u> and <u>B's</u> on her grade report.

3. After we return from our <u>month's</u> vacation, <u>we'll</u> respond to all the mail and phone messages.

4. Our cat wants <u>its</u> food in a secluded area, whereas our dogs want <u>theirs</u> in the family room.

5. No one <u>wants</u> to live in a vegetative state, unable to eat, walk, or communicate.

6. Therefore, members of the family should be the <u>ones</u> to make the critical medical decision instead of the doctors.

7. The problem is that a <u>doctor's</u> word should not be allowed to override the <u>family's</u> decision regarding a loved one.

8. Because Sirkku put too many <u>0's</u> on the bill, the accounting clerk wrote a check for $100,000 instead of $1,000.

9. <u>There's</u> never enough time to complete all of the homework assignments in Mr. <u>Buchanan's</u> class.

10. Bonnie will buy her shirt in the <u>children's</u> department because <u>it's</u> less expensive than one from the <u>women's</u> department.

Chapter 39: Quotation Marks

Answers to Chapter Review Test

1. "If you want to sell your house more quickly," the realtor advised, "paint the interior and keep the yard mowed."

2. Correct.

3. She also suggested that we read "How to Sell Your Home for the Best Price," an article in last month's *Consumer Reports.*

4. "Do you think we should have the carpets and drapes cleaned?" my mother asked.

5. "Don't bother to read Chapter Three, class," the teacher announced. "You will only be tested on Chapters Two and Four."

6. One student bravely raised his hand and asked, "Can we use our text-books or notes during the test?"

7. I read the chapter titled "The Toxicity of Lead" three times before I understood it.

8. "One of my favorite albums is Red Hot & Blue. It is a tribute album to Cole Porter by a variety of modern singers," Michelle said.

9. Correct.

10. Perhaps we would have heard the doorbell if we had not been listening to k.d. lang singing Cole Porter's song "So in Love."

Chapter 40: Other Punctuation

Answers to Chapter Review Test

1. Health issues—ranging from nutrition to exercise to disease—have progressively invaded our homes and our everyday lives.

2. Driving in our cars (a major part of our daily schedule), we see billboards promoting items that relate to health.

3. While flying down the highway, we might hear on the radio about a two-for-one special at a health club or maybe a diet cola jingle.

4. Another place for such information would be on restaurant menus, where we might find sections for people with special dietary concerns: low fat, low sodium, low cholesterol.

5. Nutrition—including the types and amounts of food that we eat—plays a big role in one way of staying healthy.

6. More nutritional foods that appeal to a large number of people (salads, vegetable platters, diet drinks) can now be found on most menus.

7. In addition, most every food product we buy in the grocery store has a list of nutritional facts on the outer label: size and number of servings, fat content, number of calories, and amounts of carbohydrates and protein.

8. Television provides the most common source of information; there we can see cooking shows that emphasize healthy cooking and paid programs for home exercise equipment.

9. Public service announcements appear on radio and television and in magazines promoting good habits and healthy lifestyles; for instance, they warn against drug abuse, heavy smoking, and drinking and driving.

10. With such widespread illustrations, it is easy to conclude that America has become a health-conscious nation.

Chapter 41: Capitalization

Answers to Chapter Review Test

1. Vacations offer a wide variety of opportunities whether you are traveling in Europe, North or South America, Asia, or the United States.

2. Between June and August, you can take a week-long cruise between Sitka and Juneau, Alaska, to view humpback whales, otters, seals, and glaciers.

3. If you vacation in Denali National Park, you can enjoy river rafting, nature hikes, cruises among the glaciers, and minibus tours.

4. My aunt and uncle enjoyed their fourteen-day Caribbean cruise that included visits to Martinique and St. Martin and lots of Creole food.

5. One of my favorite vacation spots is Colorado Springs, where I can visit natural wonders such as Seven Falls and Pike's Peak.

6. While visiting Washington, D.C., you need to see the famous monuments, the White House, and Ford's Theatre.

7. A short train ride out of Boston will take you to the church that contains crypts of President John Adams and President John Quincy Adams.

8. If you have children, you might consider a trip to Florida for fun times at Disney World, Sea World, and Universal Studios.

9. For the person who likes to shop, Mall of the Americas in Minneapolis provides the world's largest selection of shops under one roof, as well as restaurants, a skating rink, a huge Lego display, and an amusement park.

10. You can find great information for travel in publications such as *National Geographic* and from organizations such as a local chamber of commerce and the American Automobile Association.

Supplemental Exercises for Editing Chapters
(*Chapters 22–41*)

Chapter 22: The Basic Sentence—Editing Overview

22-1: Identifying Sentence Parts

For each of the following sentences, identify the word in **boldface** type as a subject, verb, adjective, adverb, conjunction, pronoun, or preposition.

EXAMPLE

adjective **Many** people are skeptical about hypnotism.

_____ 1. Can a **person** really be hypnotized?

_____ 2. Certain people **respond** very well to suggestion.

_____ 3. A person **under** hypnosis may appear not to feel pain.

_____ 4. **Hypnotized** subjects usually do what the hypnotist asks them to do.

_____ 5. People will not do things under hypnosis that they would not **normally** do.

_____ 6. **While** they are under hypnosis, some people seem to recall past lives.

_____ 7. However, the evidence **suggests** that these subjects are remembering things that they have read about.

_____ 8. Hypnosis does not **necessarily** make people tell the truth.

_____ 9. How does **hypnosis** work?

_____ 10. Hypnosis may actually affect a person's consciousness, or **it** may work because people want to cooperate with the hypnotist.

22-2: Identifying Sentence Parts

Identify the part of the sentence that is in **boldface** type. For verbs, distinguish between action verbs, linking verbs, and helping verbs. For phrases and clauses, distinguish between independent clauses, dependent clauses, and prepositional phrases.

EXAMPLE

linking verb Jellyfish **are** strange and sometimes beautiful sea creatures.

_____ 1. Jellyfish **have** existed for over 650 million years.

_____ 2. They have no eyes or ears, and **they also lack a brain and a heart.**

_____ 3. **Jellyfish have stinging tentacles,** and some jellyfish can injure humans.

_____ 4. The largest jellyfish, the lion's mane, has tentacles that **can be** one hundred feet long.

_____ 5. The tentacles trap and paralyze small sea animals **so that the jellyfish can eat them.**

_____ 6. The movement **of another swimming creature** causes the stinging cells in the tentacles of a jellyfish to fire.

_____ 7. Swimmers often **fear** jellyfish.

_____ 8. **Although jellyfish stings occasionally kill humans,** some jellyfish can actually benefit people.

_____ 9. Scientists **have** used drugs made from jellyfish to treat cancer and heart disease.

_____ 10. Medical research **may** find more uses for jellyfish in the future.

Chapter 23: Fragments—Incomplete Sentences

23-1: Correcting Fragments

In the following items, correct the fragments by connecting them to the previous or next sentence or by adding words.

EXAMPLE

Some people like to move frequently. ^f^Finding excitement in a new job in a new town. They enjoy the challenge.

1. Such people may also enjoy living in different places. Going from one part of the country to another. They can adapt.

2. Moving frequently is not easy. For everyone. Some people like familiar places and situations.

3. Even close relatives may disagree about whether to move from place to place. Or stay in one town. For example, my sister and I.

4. I have always lived in the same neighborhood. My apartment is near my parents' house. Which makes me feel safe and comfortable.

5. I like living near the house. Where I grew up. I still have many old friends in the area.

6. My sister, on the other hand. Has lived in four apartments in the last ten years. One in California, one in Chicago, and two in the Boston area.

7. Her work allows flexibility. In addition, traveling and meeting new people. For her, moving is an adventure.

8. I find it difficult. To make new friends. Moving to a strange town would be torture for me.

9. I also hate packing. Boxing up all my belongings would take a long time. Since I am a pack rat.

10. My sister and I have very different views. About the ideal way to live. Fortunately, we do not have to choose the same kind of life.

23-2: Correcting Fragments

In the following items, correct the fragments by connecting them to the previous or next sentence or by adding the missing sentence element.

EXAMPLE

Ice shelves are large masses of floating ice/~~T~~hat surround Antarctica.

1. Summer comes to the Southern Hemisphere in December. Making the weather warmest there in February and March.

2. Between late January and early March of 2002. Antarctica was experiencing the warmest summer ever recorded on the icy continent.

3. To see whether the world is really getting warmer. Scientists study the ice around the Antarctic continent carefully.

4. In the Antarctic summer of 2002. Scientists were watching an ice shelf known as Larsen B. Which is on the eastern coast of Antarctica.

5. In most places, the Larsen B ice shelf was about 220 meters thick. But melting in the unusually warm temperatures that summer.

6. Between January 31 and March 5, 2002, the Larsen B shelf lost chunks of ice totaling more than 3,200 square kilometers. A mass the size of Rhode Island.

7. Scientists around the world were stunned. At the speed of the shelf's breakup.

8. Although climate researchers do not know the exact age of the Larsen B shelf. It has probably existed for at least two thousand years.

9. The average annual temperature in the area around the Larsen B ice shelf has increased by several degrees. Since the late 1940s.

10. Scientists disagree about the reason for the shelf's disintegration. Some saying that the melting ice on top of the shelf caused the breakup, and others blaming cracks from the bottom of the shelf.

Chapter 24: Run-Ons—Two Sentences Joined Incorrectly

24-1: Correcting Run-Ons

In the following items, correct the run-ons by adding a period, a conjunction, a semicolon, or a dependent word. Add a comma if necessary. If the original sentence is correct, write "C" next to it.

EXAMPLE

Many people dread public speaking *because* they become nervous when standing in front of a large audience.

1. A survey once asked people to identify their greatest fear, the number-one answer was "public speaking."

2. The fact that the second most common response was "death" indicates how much many people dread giving speeches.

3. Many college students have to speak in front of their classmates in fact, many schools require a public-speaking class.

4. Even experienced public speakers are often nervous before a speech being nervous is not necessarily bad.

5. A feeling of nervousness can make a speaker perform well, it means that the person cares about doing a good job.

6. Of course, too much nervousness can overwhelm people, making them feel as if they are about to collapse.

7. A speech teacher or a professional speaker can offer some hints one suggestion is for the speaker to imagine the audience in their underwear.

8. Picturing such a ridiculous sight, few people can continue to be terribly nervous.

9. A speaker gets up in front of a crowd he or she may not be able to imagine a funny sight.

10. Planning for nervousness before giving a speech is good common sense it allows speakers to figure out a way to solve the problem while they are thinking calmly.

24-2: Correcting Run-Ons

In the following items, correct the run-ons by adding a period, a conjunction, a semicolon, or a dependent word. Add or delete commas if necessary.

EXAMPLE

Being a working mother is difficult, since work and school schedules often conflict.

1. More and more women in the United States are achieving career success, women with high salaries are less likely than other women to have children.

2. Half of American women who earn over one hundred thousand dollars a year are childless men who earn high salaries are no less likely than other men to have children.

3. In the business world, both male and female workers put in long hours to get ahead then they find it difficult to make time to raise a family.

4. Many male executives are married to women who raise their young children, female executives are less likely to have a partner who is willing to stay at home.

5. Of course, some women decide not to have any children, many female executives say, however, that they simply ran out of time.

6. Some businesswomen advise younger women to plan ahead women, they say, must make arrangements in advance if they want children.

7. Some younger career women believe that they will not have the same problems as previous generations women today often become successful at an earlier age.

8. A thirty-year-old woman with a good career may feel that she can take some time off, twenty years ago, few career women of childbearing age were comfortable with such a decision.

9. Young people today are frequently unconcerned about which partner earns more they also tend to be flexible about which parent stays home with the children.

10. Some powerful American women today regret being childless perhaps in the future most career women who want children will have them.

Chapter 25: Problems with Subject–Verb Agreement— When Subjects and Verbs Don't Match

25-1: Correcting Subject-Verb Agreement Problems

In the following sentences, circle the subject (or compound subject) and underline the correct form of the verb in parentheses.

EXAMPLE

(Emotions and physical responses) (is, <u>are</u>) so closely related that it is difficult to determine which occurs first.

1. (Do, Does) a person feel fear because her heart is pounding?

2. According to some psychologists, we (is, are) likely to feel afraid after experiencing a physical symptom of fear, such as a pounding heart.

3. Psychological studies have found that someone who loses the ability to feel anything from the neck down (experiences, experience) many emotions, such as anger, less strongly than before.

4. Everyone (does, do) not agree on this issue.

5. A pounding heart and a feeling of fear (happens, happen) at the same time, some psychologists say.

6. The pounding of the heart (does, do) not cause fear, they argue.

7. They argue that emotions such as fear, elation, and being in love (is, are) all characterized by a pounding heart.

8. How (do, does) people know what emotion to feel when their hearts pound?

9. Other psychologists studying emotion (believe, believes) that our minds need to identify the emotion before we feel anything.

10. Nobody knows exactly how an emotion and a physical reaction (are, is) related.

25-2: Correcting Subject–Verb Agreement Problems

For each of the sentences below, fill in the blank with the correct present-tense form of the verb in parentheses.

EXAMPLE

There ____*are*____ (is) many similarities between humans and apes.

1. One of the unusual physical features shared by humans and apes _____ (be) the thumb.

2. A person and a chimpanzee _____ (have) similar hands.

3. On our hands, the four fingers and the thumb _____ (point) in different directions.

4. Thumbs pointing in different directions than the fingers _____ (be) known as opposable thumbs.

5. Nothing _____ (make) holding and carrying things easier than an opposable thumb.

6. A person under the age of twenty-five years _____ (be) likely to use the thumb more than an older person does.

7. Younger people today _____ (have) unusually strong and flexible thumbs.

8. An explanation for these "superthumbs" _____ (be) that young people use mobile phones and other small handheld devices much more than older people do.

9. Thumbs _____ (be) positioned so that they can push buttons on handheld devices more easily than index fingers can.

10. Among young people today, pointing at an object and ringing a doorbell _____ (be) becoming jobs for the thumb rather than for the index finger.

Chapter 26: Verb Problems—Mistakes in Verb Form and Verb Tense

26-1: Using Correct Verb Forms and Tenses

For each of the sentences below, fill in the blank with the correct form and tense of the verb in parentheses.

EXAMPLE

Driving ___is___ (be) a privilege that can be taken away from reckless drivers.

1. Last year, Sandra _____ (lose) her driver's license.

2. She _____ (drive) recklessly for several years before she had an accident.

3. The accident _____ (hurt) Sandra slightly.

4. Fortunately, no one else _____ (be) injured.

5. Sandra _____ (have) a suspended license for fourteen months now.

6. Now she _____ (want) to get her license again.

7. Sandra told me that she _____ (find) information about getting an international driver's license through a Web site that asks no questions about your driving record.

8. I had never heard of using an international driver's license to replace a suspended license, and I _____ (tell) Sandra so.

9. It _____ (turn) out that the international driver's license offer was a scam.

10. To get her license back, Sandra now _____ (go) to a state-approved driving course on the weekends.

26-2: Using Correct Verb Forms and Tenses

For each of the following sentences, underline the correct form and tense of the verb in parentheses.

EXAMPLE

Two hundred years ago, England (<u>controlled</u>, had controlled) many colonies in Africa.

1. When the English arrived in Africa, they (brought, bring) many traditions that still exist there today.

2. The British (introduced, had introduced) their legal and political systems to their African colonies.

3. Since then, most African countries (gained, have gained) their independence.

4. However, through decades of independence, many African judges and lawyers (continued, have continued) the British tradition of wearing horsehair wigs in court.

5. Today, some people (saw, see) the tradition as ridiculous.

6. After all, until the British colonized Africa, no African (wore, had worn) a horsehair wig.

7. However, Africans wearing the wigs (had earned, have earned) their high positions after years of study and hard work.

8. Over the years, judges and lawyers (become, have become) used to wearing the wigs and demanding respect for them.

9. Recently, a member of the National Assembly of Kenya (called, had called) on other Kenyan politicians to adopt a more traditional African style of dress.

10. He (put, has put) on an embroidered robe to encourage others to dress more traditionally.

Chapter 27: Pronouns—Using Substitutes for Nouns

27-1: Correcting Errors in Pronoun Use

Edit the following sentences to ensure that the proper pronoun is used. If a sentence is already correct, write "C" next to it.

EXAMPLE

Though Web sites can be very useful, it is important to evaluate ~~its~~ *their* reliability.

1. Anyone using their computer to go online has seen Web sites that contain advertising.

2. A student who uses the Internet should know that some information online is not reliable.

3. However, many people, they do not realize that some online information that seems reliable comes from advertisers.

4. When my sister did an online search, they gave her results from sites that paid to be mentioned.

5. Her and I had not known that advertisers could influence a search engine.

6. This information was rather shocking to her and me.

7. An organization called Consumers Union announced their intention to help Internet users get accurate information.

8. My sister and her boyfriend got his or her information about evaluating a Web site's trustworthiness from the Consumers Union.

9. The Consumers Union site said that a Web site should identify whom created it and where it is produced.

10. Unless Web sites follow guidelines, a consumer is likely to find that he or she continues to have difficulty telling online advertising and editorial content apart.

27-2: Correcting Errors in Pronoun Use

Edit the following sentences to correct the errors in pronoun use.

EXAMPLE

A teenaged girl and a teenaged boy can both act aggressively toward ~~his or her~~ *their*

peers at times.

1. However, males and females vent his or her anger in different ways.

2. My brother and me had very different experiences in high school, but we both had some trouble with other teenagers.

3. My brother was much more likely than me to get into a physical fight with someone.

4. According to recent research, they say that girls tend to disguise their aggression.

5. A girl whom gets angry with another girl is not likely to have a physical fight with her.

6. Instead, a girl will probably try to hurt another girl psychologically; this happened to my friends and I in high school.

7. Everyone in my group of friends had their turn at being an outsider.

8. When I was an outsider, my friends insulted my clothes and hair or revealed secrets you had told them.

9. My brother and his best friend had his arguments, but they never resorted to the kind of treachery and insults that my friends and I inflicted on one another.

10. No one is certain why girls behave this way, but anyone who had their female friends turn on them in high school remembers how painful the experience was.

Chapter 28: Adjectives and Adverbs— Describing *Which One?* or *How?*

28-1: Using Adjectives and Adverbs Correctly

In the following sentences, underline the correct adjective or adverb in parentheses.

EXAMPLE

Technology can revolutionize our society in ways that (great, greatly, more greatly) influence our daily lives.

1. In the future, cars may be able to help drivers reach home (safe, safely, safest).

2. In order to drive (well, good, better), a person needs to be awake and alert.

3. Everyone knows that driving a car can sometimes make a person (sleepy, sleepily, sleepier).

4. The motion of the car and the boredom of a familiar stretch of highway can be a (more dangerous, dangerous, dangerously) combination.

5. Most busy people today do not get enough rest, so drivers today are (likeliest, likely, likelier) than in the past to fall asleep at the wheel.

6. Car designers have been seeking the (good, better, best) way for a car to identify and alert a tired driver.

7. Someday, a car may (sudden, most sudden, suddenly) ask the driver a question.

8. If a driver responds (slower, slowly, more slowly) than the car is programmed to expect, the driver is probably falling asleep.

9. The car of the future may splash a sleepy driver with water, which would be unpleasant, but certainly no (bad, worse, worst) than falling asleep and having an accident.

10. Technology can certainly help human beings in everyday life, but the (most effective, effectively, effective) method of staying awake while driving is still to get enough sleep before getting in the car.

28-2: Correcting Errors in Adjective and Adverb Use

Edit the following sentences to correct any errors in adjective or adverb use. If the sentence is already correct, write a "C" next to it.

EXAMPLE

Television advertisers have ~~traditional~~ *traditionally* been willing to pay a lot to reach the ~~desirablest~~ *most desirable* consumers.

1. Advertisers think that targeting people in their teens and twenties will make products sell good.

2. Businesses therefore frequently compete for the chance to reach those audiences.

3. Because many businesses are hopefully that showing commercials during television shows with young adult viewers will improve sales, advertising time on those shows is among the more expensivest on television.

4. A show with an audience made up almost totally of teenagers and young adults may do pretty badly in the overall ratings.

5. Instead of being canceled quick, such a show can make a profit by attracting advertisers who pay better-than-average rates for the commercial time on the show.

6. Advertisers are certainly that it is more easier to influence a young audience than a middle-aged one.

7. Advertisers believe that older audiences are loyaller to products than younger ones are, so businesses see an older person as a badder customer for a new product.

8. Are youthfuller audiences more likely than older ones to be real interested in trying new brands?

9. According to research, a typically middle-aged customer tries new brands more willingly than a teenager tries them, so paying extra money to reach young customers is probably a badly idea.

10. In spite of this fact, advertisers have been surprisingly uninterested in changing their methods and targeting middle-aged people who might be persuaded fairly easily to try a new product.

Chapter 29: Misplaced and Dangling Modifiers— Avoiding Confusing Descriptions

29-1: Identifying Misplaced and Dangling Modifiers

In the following items, indicate whether the word group in **boldface** type is a misplaced modifier, a dangling modifier, or a correctly placed modifier. In the space provided, write an "M" (for misplaced), a "D" (for dangling) or a "C" (for correct).

EXAMPLE

_____M_____ Ants often fight to protect their nest or food resources, **small but aggressive insects.**

_____ 1. In its native country, the Argentine ant forms small colonies, **a tiny black species of ant.**

_____ 2. **Attacking other insects, including other Argentine ants, in Argentina,** scientists were surprised recently to find huge Argentine ant colonies in Europe and North America.

_____ 3. The European ant colony is one giant cooperative unit **stretching for 3,500 miles along the Mediterranean.**

_____ 4. **The largest cooperative of any kind in the world,** scientists are astonished at the ants' ability to get along peacefully.

_____ 5. **Investigating the ants' ability to cooperate,** scientists have looked at the ants' genetic makeup.

_____ 6. Did a very small number of ants reach Europe **that were genetically alike?**

_____ 7. Ants may react to each other without violence **from closely related colonies.**

_____ 8. Other scientists suggest that colonies **genetically inclined to get along with other colonies** survived and grew because they spent less time fighting.

_____ 9. Small colonies **only** containing a few cooperative ants might have grown into an enormous peaceful colony.

_____ 10. The Argentine ants may have lessons to teach, **observing the ants' ability to change from vicious enemies to peaceful neighbors.**

29-2: Correcting Misplaced and Dangling Modifiers

Edit the following sentences to eliminate problems with misplaced and dangling modifiers. It may be necessary to add or change words.

EXAMPLE

Filling out an application for college, many ~~schools require~~ an admissions essay.

students are required to write ^

1. Every student nearly struggles to write a convincing admissions essay.

2. A student might even seek help with his or her essay who is a strong writer.

3. At some schools, admissions officers have begun to ask students to describe the writing help they received, wondering if the essays are actually written by applicants.

4. At one prominent university, the essay form says that "all good writers seek feedback, advice, or editing" that all students must complete.

5. A few students write their essays without help who are very confident of their writing skills.

6. If those students report that they did not get any assistance truthfully, will admissions committees think that they are lying?

7. Of course, seeking input is always a good idea before submitting written work.

8. Not wanting to give the wrong impression, anyone from a friend to a professional may be consulted for help with an important piece of writing.

9. Admissions officers say that they need to know how much is a student's own work of the admissions essay.

10. While trying to make the admissions process fair to students who play by the rules, students continue to feel that they are under tremendous pressure when they apply to colleges.

Chapter 30: Coordination and Subordination—Joining Ideas

30-1: Using Coordination or Subordination to Join Two Sentences

Combine each of the following pairs of sentences by using either coordination or subordination.

EXAMPLE

Wolves are beautiful animals*, but they*/~~They~~ cause problems for sheep and cattle ranchers.

1. Wolves were once part of the landscape in many western states. They were killed off in the twentieth century.

2. Wild wolves from Canada were released in Montana and Wyoming in the mid-1990s. Many people were pleased to have wolves back in the western United States.

3. Many ranchers objected to the return of the wolves. They feared for the safety of their livestock.

4. The wolves were endangered. Hunting them was illegal.

5. Unhappy ranchers opposed the wolves' presence. The government promised to kill any wolf that harmed livestock.

6. Ranchers demanded compensation for animals killed by wolves. Environmental groups agreed to pay for livestock losses.

7. Wolf policies became controversial in 2002. The government paid for the killing of an entire wolf pack.

8. The government spent fifteen thousand dollars to hunt down the pack. The wolves killed just a few hundred dollars worth of livestock.

9. The wolves were wearing radio collars. Government hunters were able to track and kill the wolves with the help of those collars.

10. A wildlife organization had donated the collars to help biologists. The group decided not to provide any more radio collars.

30-2: Using Coordination or Subordination to Join Two Sentences

Combine each of the following pairs of sentences by using either coordination or subordination.

EXAMPLE

Pieces of rock frequently fly through space at very high speeds. The pieces burn. *; as a result, the*

1. These meteors are visible on a clear night. They have been admired by stargazers for thousands of years.

2. Sometimes they burn up completely in space. At other times, they fall to earth.

3. Ancient Romans worshipped the meteorites that landed on earth. They considered them "stones from heaven."

4. Later observers were more skeptical. Scientists in the eighteenth century did not believe meteorites existed.

5. A meteor shower happened in broad daylight in France in 1803. Most people began to believe in the reality of meteorites.

6. Meteorites tend to land most often in just a few places. In the United States, the most meteorites are in Texas, Kansas, New Mexico, and Colorado.

7. Australia and Antarctica are rich in meteorites. The Sahara Desert may be the best place on earth for locating them.

8. Meteorites contain a great deal of iron. Some people use magnets to find them.

9. Meteorites are often darkly colored or strangely marked. Collectors pay high prices for them.

10. One collector recently sold a rare specimen. He received two million dollars for it.

Chapter 31: Parallelism—Balancing Ideas

31-1: Correcting Errors in Parallelism

Edit the following sentences to make them parallel. If an item is already parallel, write "C" next to it.

EXAMPLE

Immigrants in a new land often like buying familiar ingredients, ~~to cook~~ *cooking* traditional foods, and ~~they eat~~ *eating* the things they remember from home.

1. In the United States, immigrants in many areas have not only neighbors from their native country but they can also shop at markets with familiar foods.

2. In the past, many immigrants found that small ethnic markets served their needs better than shopping at large supermarkets.

3. Supermarkets are now trying to attract shoppers by selling ethnic produce, mainly from Asia, Central American, and South American countries.

4. For many shoppers, finding everything in one store is better than to get a few items in one place and the rest in another.

5. Many customers realize that supermarkets have the advantage of low prices, a large selection of items, and convenience.

6. If an immigrant cannot buy both ethnic food and American items at the supermarket, that customer might prefer to shop at smaller, specialized stores.

7. On the other hand, if a customer can buy both ethnic food and can get milk, eggs, and shampoo at the same supermarket, the supermarket may win a loyal shopper.

8. Supermarkets lose money and business if they stock items that people do not want or by failing to stock items that customers demand.

9. In areas with many immigrants, supermarkets are learning that offering ethnic foods is a better economic decision than ignoring the tastes of immigrants.

10. Ethnic foods, such as Indian, and dishes from Thailand, are also becoming increasingly popular among nonimmigrant Americans.

31-2: Correcting Errors in Parallelism

Edit the following sentences to make them parallel.

EXAMPLE

It is difficult to balance family, ~~going to~~ work, and household chores.

1. Chores such as doing the laundry, cleaning the house, and the dishes take time even when people use modern appliances to help.

2. Many people feel that household jobs are not only boring but they are also time-consuming.

3. Twenty years ago, many people believed that men and women would soon share household chores equally, spend the same amount of time with their children, and that both would work outside the home.

4. However, most working husbands today neither do half of the housework nor do they spend as much time with their children as most working wives do.

5. Wives in 1965 most often stayed at home and raising children full-time.

6. Today, when a majority of young and middle-aged wives work outside the home, women, on average, spend twice as much time doing housework as the hours spent by men.

7. Many people, both men and women, view doing housework as less important than an office job.

8. Although Americans say that children are very important, many people respect a position outside the home more than a person who stays home to care for children.

9. Will the next generation of young men do more housework and helping raise the children?

10. If today's boys are to grow up to do their fair share of work at home, their parents must teach them the importance of that work, make them see that housework is the responsibility of both husbands and wives, and the parents need to set a good example.

Chapter 32: Sentence Variety—Putting Rhythm in Your Writing

32-1: Improving Sentence Variety

Edit the following pairs of sentences to create better sentence variety. Use the techniques covered in this chapter: Start a sentence with an *-ly* adverb, or join sentences by using an *-ing* word, *-ed* word, appositive, or adjective clause that begins with *who, which,* or *that*. In many cases, there is more than one way to combine the sentences.

EXAMPLE

Obesity is a disease/It increases a person's risk of developing high blood pressure, diabetes, and heart disease.

that

1. Obesity is an increasing problem in the United States. It affects one out of eight American schoolchildren.

2. Researchers see many reasons for widespread obesity. They blame factors such as fast food, parents, schools, and advertisements.

3. Fast-food restaurants are a major source of fat in the American diet. They offer larger portions now than in previous decades.

4. French fries at McDonald's are one example. They now appear in a "super size" that is three times as large as the portion sold in 1955.

5. Children also pick up bad eating habits at home. They are often surrounded with junk food and soft drinks instead of healthy snacks.

6. Many parents mean well. They teach their children to prize candy and desserts by using them as rewards or special treats.

7. Schools are not teaching good nutrition either. They often allow snack and soft drink companies to advertise or sell products inside the school.

8. Schoolchildren are bombarded with food advertising at home and at school. They often give in to advertisements even if they do not want or need the food.

9. Physical activity is an important way to fight obesity. It is no longer a significant part of everyday life for many children.

10. Obesity is a major cause of premature death in this country. It will become a larger problem if today's overweight children become overweight adults.

32-2: Improving Sentence Variety

Edit the following pairs of sentences to create better sentence variety. Use the techniques covered in this chapter: Start a sentence with an -*ly* adverb, or join sentences by using an -*ing* word, -*ed* word, appositive, or adjective clause that begins with *who, which,* or *that*. In many cases, there is more than one way to combine the sentences.

EXAMPLE

My grandmother ~~is~~ *, who is* seventy-four years old/. ~~She~~ loves the Internet.

1. Email is her greatest delight. It allows her to keep in touch with her grandchildren.

2. Her hearing is getting worse with time. It prevents her from understanding some spoken words.

3. My grandmother is frustrated by many telephone conversations these days. She loves having another way to contact friends and family quickly.

4. She has stopped listening to television and radio newscasters. They don't provide information that is useful to her.

5. My grandmother is a diabetic. She finds out about the latest treatments and research online.

6. She is fascinated with opera. She has found dozens of Web sites about her favorite singers and composers.

7. Americans over age sixty-five are the fastest-growing segment of the population. They have not generally been quick to adapt to the computer age.

8. Older women want to communicate with loved ones and find information. They are taking up computing faster than any other group of people in the United States.

9. My grandmother remains young at heart. She sees the Internet as a way of keeping in touch with the most enjoyable parts of her life.

10. However, she hasn't yet adapted to cellular phones. Cellular phones are another product of the technology age.

Chapter 33: ESL Concerns—Areas of Special Interest to Nonnative Speakers

33-1: ESL Concerns Review

Edit the following sentences to eliminate any problems with nouns and articles, verbs, prepositions, negative statements, and questions. If the original sentence contains no errors, write a "C" next to it.

EXAMPLE

~~The~~ P̷ollution is a worldwide problem that everyone should be worried ~~of~~ *about*.

1. For the many years, Americans have not worried much about pollution in the other countries.

2. However, scientists who study the atmosphere now understand that dangerous pollution from Asia and Africa can reach the United States.

3. Dust enormous storms in China are causing high levels of smog on the American West Coast.

4. Chinese farmers keep using many dangerous chemicals that not are allowed in the United States.

5. Dust storms can pick out these chemicals in China and carry them across the Pacific Ocean.

6. Americans on the East Coast cannot expect to avoid dangerous dust from abroad.

7. Dust storms in western Africa may be responsible for an increase in pollution in Florida and other parts of the United States.

8. A scientist who investigating African dust in the United States has found viruses in the dust.

9. Did viruses migrated from Africa to the United States on particles of dust?

10. It is seeming that Americans will soon have to care on pollution problems around the world.

33-2: ESL Concerns Review

Edit the following sentences to eliminate any problems with nouns and articles, verbs, prepositions, negative statements, and questions. If the original sentence contains no errors, write a "C" next to it.

EXAMPLE

Is owning
~~Owning~~ a car ~~is~~ worth the expense?
  ^

1. People in many parts of the world expect paying much higher prices for gasoline than Americans do.

2. In the United States, gasoline low prices surprise visitors from Europe and Asia.

3. However, most Americans with cars are knowing how expensive owning a car can be.

4. In much of a this country, people spend almost as much money on transportation as they spend on housing.

5. For most people, filling out the gas tank is usually only a small part of the cost of car ownership.

6. A person who buys a car may not be aware about the other expenses involved, such as insurance, car payments, and repairs.

7. Because the cost of living in many cities is so high, the people in much of the country live in homes many miles from their jobs.

8. They live in areas that do not have no public transportation.

9. Suburban housing not costs as much as living in town, but the cost of owning a car can make the suburbs more expensive.

10. A person thinking of moving far from town to a place where housing is inexpensive should get some advices about the cost of transportation.

Chapter 34: Word Choice—Avoiding Language Pitfalls

34-1: Improving Word Choice

Rewrite the following sentences to eliminate the four language pitfalls covered in Chapter 34: vague and abstract words, slang, wordiness, and clichés.

EXAMPLE

Because many
~~Due to the fact that a great number of~~ Americans are too rushed for time to
^

prepare a healthy meal, the United States has come to be known as the "fast-food nation."

1. Many Americans pig out on junk food way too often.

2. According to a recent study of the types and kinds of foods consumed by residents of the United States, almost half of the meals prepared in the kitchens of America are vegetable-deficient.

3. It is not crystal clear whether the study of the American diet counted potato chips as a member of the family of vegetables.

4. Americans scarf down more potato chips than any other snack food, over a billion pounds a year.

5. Although the potato was once originally a native South American food item, the fact of the matter is that the potato chip was the creation of a chef who cooked in Saratoga Springs, New York.

6. In addition, it is considered true that the ice cream cone and the hamburger were invented in the United States.

7. Here's a shocker: fortune cookies and chop suey, big in Chinese restaurants, were also created in the United States.

8. The Popsicle and the Twinkie, which are beloved and adored by American children in this day and age and in the past, were also invented in this country.

9. Americans also beat the world's food industry to the punch by creating prepared mixes; the first one down the pike was a pancake mix.

10. With the enormous potential of convenience foods, another American innovation, in developing markets on a global scale around the world, should Americans be filled with pride at their contribution to world cuisine?

34-2: Improving Word Choice

Rewrite the following sentences to eliminate the four language pitfalls covered in Chapter 34: vague and abstract words, slang, wordiness, and clichés.

EXAMPLE

Americans, who work ~~like dogs~~, spend very little time on leisure activities.
(long hours)

1. At this point in time, Americans have less vacation time than people in any other industrialized country have.

2. On average, the boss of an American company gives the wage slaves just thirteen days out of each year as vacation time.

3. Thirteen days is a drop in the bucket compared to the average number of vacation days in Italy.

4. Italian workers are the recipients of an average of forty-two days of vacation time on an annual basis.

5. Europeans in general get a whopping amount of vacation time, with French and German workers averaging thirty-six days a year and British workers getting twenty-eight.

6. Most Americans will never in a million years get a month off from work every year.

7. Even in Japan, where employees are noted for putting their nose to the grindstone for long hours, the average vacation time is twenty-five days per year.

8. The sorriest thing about all of this is that many Americans don't even go for the vacations they have coming to them.

9. One out of six U.S. workers fails to use annual vacation time due to the fact that he or she feels obliged to remain on hand at work instead.

10. Doctors say that vacations are good for people's health.

Chapter 35: Commonly Confused Words— Avoiding Mistakes with Sound-alikes

35-1: Using the Right Word

In the following sentences, underline the correct word from the choices in parentheses.

EXAMPLE

Lately, I have had to (right, <u>write</u>) things down in order to remember them.

1. When I forget things, I sometimes feel as if I am (loosing, losing) my memory.

2. My (mine, mind) plays tricks on me, especially when I am under stress.

3. In many of my classes, I am (supposed, suppose) to learn information by heart.

4. Sometimes I just (set, sit) and stare at the material my professors tell me to learn.

5. I know that (they're, their) not trying to torture me, but sometimes it feels that way.

6. (It's, Its) strangely comforting to know that other students have the same problem.

7. When I took French last year, everyone in the class was getting terrible grades (except, accept) one student, my friend Keith.

8. I would (of, have) had a hard time passing my foreign language requirement if Keith had not taught me a clever trick for memorizing words.

9. He said that I should make a (conscience, conscious) effort to picture a phrase associated with the word I was trying to remember, and soon I was picturing myself chatting with a cat to remember that *chat* is French for cat.

10. I have used Keith's (advice, advise) in many other situations since then, and the trick has helped me remember names, facts, and all kinds of important things.

35-2: Using the Right Word

In the following sentences, correct any words that are used incorrectly. Some sentences may contain more than one error.

EXAMPLE

The largest woodpecker in America ~~use~~ *used* to be the ivory-billed woodpecker, which measured twenty inches from ~~it's~~ *its* head to ~~it's~~ *its* tail.

1. Ivory-billed woodpeckers were once known too live in U.S. forests, though none has been documented by bird experts since the 1940s.

2. Has the ivory-billed woodpecker past into extinction, or has it simply hidden for decades without being observed?

3. The reported sighting of an ivory-billed woodpecker buy a credible source in 1999 had the affect of sending scientists to Louisiana to look for the bird.

4. Recordings of ivory-billed woodpeckers where made in the 1930s, so to-day's scientists new what to listen for.

5. When this woodpecker wraps on a tree, the knocking sounds come in pairs, and it's call sounds like a toy trumpet.

6. Teams of ornithologists—scientists who's specialty is birds—spent days in the Pearl River Wildlife Management Area in Louisiana where they watched and listened for signs of the giant woodpecker's presence.

7. On their trip, the ornithologists saw large wholes in tree trunks that could have been created by ivory-billed woodpeckers.

8. They also herd a double knocking sound, which might indicate that ivory-billed woodpeckers were there in the forest, but they never saw the birds.

9. Although the scientists did not fine ivory-billed woodpeckers on the trip, the scientists left recording devices.

10. They hope that the devices will soon tape trumpeting sounds in the quite woods.

Chapter 36: Spelling—Using the Right Letters

36-1: Correcting Spelling Mistakes

In the following sentences, correct any misspelled words. Some sentences may contain more than one spelling mistake. You may want to refer to the six spelling rules in Chapter 36.

EXAMPLE

a lot   *consuming*
In ~~alot~~ of cities around the United States, owning a car can be time-~~consumeing~~

and expensive.

1. Traditionnal businesses rent cars to people who need them in an unfamiliar city or for a weekend trip.

2. In major U.S. citys today, a new idea—shareing a vehicle—is catching on with residents who do not own cars.

3. People who particepate in a car share must pay a membership fee and meet certain requirements.

4. Convictions for drunk or wreckless driving are not allowed; having severel moving violations can also cause a driver to be rejected.

5. Members of most car-share companies recieve an electronic key card.

6. Members can then actavate the key card when they need to use a car.

7. As in a typical car rental, drivers who share usualy find it necesary to reserve a car in advance.

8. Once their cars have been reserved for a particular ocasion, however, they simply go to a garage when they are scheduled to have the car and drive off.

9. Car sharers reconize that they are making a comitment to the company and to the other owners: They have to return the car undamaged and with plenty of gas in the tank.

10. According to car-share companies, members are exellent at keeping the cars in good condition because the drivers know that they will probaly drive that same car again.

36-2: Correcting Spelling Mistakes

Each of the following sentences contains one misspelled word. Identify and correct the spelling mistake in each sentence.

EXAMPLE

Fights between siblings, ~~expecially~~ *especially* those who are close in age, are common.

1. Nearly everyone who has a brother or a sister is familiar with ocasional sibling rivalry.

2. Parents often wonder when arguements between two children have gone too far.

3. Experts beleive that siblings who fight are competing for their parents' affection.

4. Brothers and sisters tend to develope rivalries over possessions and space, such as a bedroom or a particular seat in the car.

5. Children can also compete for priveleges, which make them feel that their parents favor them.

6. Most of the time, sibling rivalry is a problem that parents find merely anoying, not actually dangerous.

7. However, parents occasionally need to seek profesional help for their children.

8. Children who fight chronicly and show no remorse for their behavior may need counseling.

9. Experts also insist that any child who uses violence against a sibling should get help imediately.

10. In general, if parents truely feel concerned, they ought to trust their own instincts and at least discuss the problem with someone.

Chapter 37: Commas

37-1: Using Commas Correctly

In the following sentences, add commas where they are needed. If the sentence is already correct, write "C" next to it.

EXAMPLE

People who feel uncomfortable with their appearance may turn to liposuction,

nose jobs, and implants to change the way they look.

1. Any treatment that promises to make people look younger is almost guaranteed to attract customers so researchers keep developing anti-aging formulas.

2. Even though most treatments are expensive they are becoming increasingly popular among men as well as women.

3. A drug called botulinum toxin a form of a paralyzing poison was approved for medical use by the Food and Drug Administration.

4. For patients with severe muscle contractions botulinum toxin was a proven treatment.

5. The word quickly spread that botulinum toxin known as "Botox" also effectively removed facial wrinkles and lines.

6. Botox was not approved for cosmetic uses yet many healthy people began asking doctors to inject them with it.

7. Faces that are treated with Botox are not permanently smoothed because the toxin wears off after a few months.

8. However after too much Botox parts of a person's face may appear strangely unable to move.

9. Side effects of Botox treatments can include headaches nausea and drooping eyelids.

10. In the spring of 2002 Botox was approved for use in cosmetic treatments a development that simply acknowledged how the drug was already being used.

37-2: Using Commas Correctly

In the following sentences, add commas where they are needed and fix misplaced commas.

EXAMPLE

Dr. Albert Abrams‸a professor of medicine‸made a fortune from his bizarre inventions.

1. Abrams who was born around 1863, was one of the most successful quacks in medical history.

2. In 1910 Abrams claimed that, he could cure diseases by tapping on a patient's spine.

3. The dawn of the electronic age arrived and, Abrams introduced electronic machines to a gullible public.

4. When Americans became fascinated, with radio, Abrams announced that he could use radios to diagnose diseases.

5. Abrams's theory of electronic diagnosis, called the Electronic Reactions of Abrams involved, an elaborate machine called a dynamizer.

6. The dynamizer analyzed, a sample of blood drawn, while a patient faced west.

7. Skeptics supplied sheep blood chicken blood, and, red ink.

8. When the dynamizer diagnosed fatal illnesses Dr. Abrams informed the skeptics, that another machine the oscilloclast, could cure them for $250.

9. After a thorough investigation of Abrams's techniques *Scientific American* called the dynamizer "utterly worthless."

10. Abrams who died on January 13 1924 fooled enough people to leave behind an estate worth $2 million.

Chapter 38: Apostrophes

38-1: Using Apostrophes Correctly

Edit the following sentences by adding apostrophes where they are needed and by crossing out any apostrophes that are used incorrectly or positioned incorrectly in the word.

EXAMPLE

My boss's home computer has been working on its own time for the last few months.

1. Shes been loaning it out to analyze a stream of 0s and 1s coming from an organization called the Search for Extraterrestrial Intelligence, or SETI.

2. SETIs giant telescope in Arecibo, Puerto Rico, scan's space for signals.

3. SETI scientist's hope that someday they will receive a signal from extraterrestrial life forms.

4. The telescopes' data contains both strong and weak signals, and theres a huge amount of data to be analyzed.

5. The SETI labs dont have a powerful enough computer to analyze all of the data quickly.

6. The scientists estimated that it could take hundred's of years to look closely at the weak signals on a less powerful computer.

7. The scientists considered the problem, and an idea of their's solved it: Theyd ask hundreds of small computers to analyze chunks of data when the computers werent doing anything else.

8. Its now quite simple for a volunteer like my boss to download a screen saver that picks up data from the SETI telescope and analyzes it.

9. When my boss doesn't need the computer to be doing work of her's, she lets it sift through the signals from space and report its analysis to SETI.

10. Maybe someday, shell be the one to help decode a message from space, and the SETI scientist's work will change the way we look at the universe.

38-2: Using Apostrophes Correctly

Edit the following sentences by adding apostrophes where they are needed and by crossing out any apostrophes that are used incorrectly or positioned incorrectly in the word.

EXAMPLE

If you've ever wanted a job using high technology, ~~its~~ *it's* time to consider the construction industry.

1. While computer programming has it's place in many offices, technological tools are also commonly found on construction site's.

2. For example, a bulldozers' blade is often controlled by electronics.

3. With computers assistance, underground tunnels for pipes can be created by machines that do'nt need to dig down from ground level.

4. While many dot-com's are going out of business, the construction industry's need for workers is increasing.

5. Analyst's projections indicate that over two million job's in construction will be unfilled in 2010.

6. With ten hours worth of overtime a week, a skilled construction worker today can make almost one hundred thousand dollars a year in some parts' of the country.

7. Construction workers skills are quickly becoming more technological.

8. Today, its' not unusual for many construction sites to use lasers and robotics.

9. Doesnt using electronics, cameras, computers, and robots to build things sound like itd be fun?

10. A job like this could be your's if youre good with technology.

Chapter 39: Quotation Marks

39-1: Using Quotation Marks Correctly

Edit the following sentences by adding quotation marks and commas where they are needed and by crossing out quotation marks and commas that are used incorrectly. Also correct any other punctuation mistakes you notice.

EXAMPLE

My six-year-old brother told me that "he didn't understand some of the words in the story he was reading."

1. I asked him "What's it called"?

2. He held up a book that had been mine, "The Collected Stories of Beatrix Potter."

3. He told me, "It's "The Tale of Peter Rabbit" by Beatrix Potter."

4. My favorite stories from the collection were "The Tale of Benjamin Bunny, The Tale of the Flopsy Bunnies, and The Tale of Mrs. Tiggy-Winkle."

5. Picking up the book, I told him show me the part of the story you don't understand.

6. It says that the sparrows "implored him to exert himself," he said.

7. How stupid did I feel when I said, "I need a dictionary to look up one of those words?"

8. My mother overheard us and told him that the sparrows wanted "Peter Rabbit" to try very hard to escape.

9. "You never seem foolish for looking up a word" she said to us.

10. She said "that I would only look foolish if I pretended to know a word that I didn't understand."

39-2: Using Quotation Marks Correctly

Edit the following sentences by adding quotation marks and commas where they are needed and by crossing out quotation marks and commas that are used incorrectly. Also correct any other punctuation mistakes you notice. If the sentence is already correct, write a "C" next to it.

EXAMPLE

My Aunt Catherine told me ⸢she couldn't believe how hard it was for her to get health insurance.⸥

1. "I'm overweight, but I'm in excellent health" she said.

2. Aunt Catherine has a nursing degree from the "Columbia College of Nursing."

3. After her husband lost his job, she contacted an insurance company and asked "how much it would cost to get a family insurance policy."

4. The letter she received said "We're sorry, but your weight puts you at risk".

5. "My cholesterol level and blood pressure are excellent, she said, and I exercise regularly."

6. She showed me a newspaper article called, "Is Obesity a Disease or Just a Symptom"?

7. "The author says right here, 'Being overweight is not necessarily life threatening," she said.

8. I told her that she should ask her doctor for proof of her good health.

9. She got a letter from him that said, Catherine is fit and will probably live to a ripe old age."

10. Aunt Catherine is still trying to find an insurance company that recognizes that "she can be both healthy and overweight."

Chapter 40: Other Punctuation

40-1: Using Colons, Semicolons, Parentheses, Dashes, and Hyphens

Edit the following sentences by adding colons, semicolons, parentheses, dashes, and hyphens where needed. You may also need to change some commas to semicolons.

EXAMPLE

Drug addiction ⁀ the mental and physical compulsion to use a drug ⁀ affects some drug users and not others.

1. Drug addiction often leads to serious medical problems it is therefore considered a disease.

2. Some people and no one knows which people are more likely than others to become addicts.

3. Diagnostic tests are not available to identify an addiction prone person.

4. A tendency toward drug addiction may be genetic, it may also be an accident of brain chemistry.

5. The drugs that cause serious addiction problems may be those substances traditionally considered most dangerous heroin, crack cocaine, and powdered cocaine.

6. However, marijuana now a much more potent drug than it was thirty years ago also causes dependence among some young people.

7. According to a 2001 poll, 40 percent of American eighteen year olds have smoked marijuana at least once.

8. Some of these young people will react to super potent marijuana by showing signs of psychological addiction needing the drug daily, needing larger and larger amounts of it, spending a lot of money and effort to get it, and lying about drug use to friends and family.

9. Some teenagers who feel that their marijuana use causes problems do quit however, over two thirds of them will start smoking it again.

10. Most teenagers do not realize that there can be long-term consequences including addiction of trying marijuana.

40-2: Using Colons, Semicolons, Parentheses, Dashes, and Hyphens

Edit the following sentences by adding colons, semicolons, parentheses, dashes, and hyphens where needed. You may also need to change some commas to semicolons.

EXAMPLE

The quagga was a yellowish brown relative of the zebra with zebra-like stripes on its head, neck, and chest.

1. Quaggas native to South Africa once roamed the plains by the thousands.

2. Boer settlers in the region killed off quaggas for several reasons the animals competed with livestock for scarce grass, they were a source of food, and their hides were striking.

3. Soon, the extinction of the quagga was complete the last wild quagga died in 1878, and the last quagga in captivity died in the Amsterdam Zoo in 1883.

4. In the 1980s, an analysis of DNA from a quagga hide showed that quaggas long considered a unique species were a subspecies of the Burchell's zebra.

5. The Hottentots of South Africa had always used the term "quagga" a word imitating the creatures' cry to name both Burchell's zebra and the extinct quagga.

6. The Quagga Project is a breeding program in South Africa scientists select Burchell's zebras for quagga like coloring and markings.

7. The program has had some success since its 1987 beginnings the zebras in the breeding program have fainter stripes on their backs and rumps, and they are noticeably browner than traditional Burchell's zebras.

8. Quagga Project scientists hope that they may be retrieving genes once found in wild quaggas there is no way to be certain since no genetic material from extinct quaggas survives.

9. The Quagga Project wants to return animals that look like the long lost quagga to the South African plains.

10. The project would not exactly bring quaggas back from extinction however, many people still hope to see the project succeed.

Chapter 41: Capitalization—Using Capital Letters

41-1: Capitalizing

Edit the following sentences by correcting errors in capitalization.

EXAMPLE

What caused the mental illness of ~~e~~ngland's ~~k~~ing George III?

(editing marks: E above the e in england's; K above the k in king)

1. An article in a British Medical Journal once suggested that the King was suffering from porphyria, a rare blood disease.

2. this idea was used in Alan Bennett's play *the madness of king george* and the movie with the same name.

3. The play and movie suggested that George's porphyria contributed to his anger at the American colonies and, therefore, to the Revolutionary war.

4. Historians have no way of knowing if the monarch's first period of insanity, during which parliament nearly declared him unfit to rule, was actually caused by porphyria, but it may have been.

5. Porphyria has also been linked by some people to the popular conception of Vampires.

6. One form of porphyria causes sufferers' skin to blister when it is exposed to the sun, so, like dracula in Bram Stoker's Novel, they stay indoors during the day.

7. The vampires of Folklore in stories from Balkan Countries, however, usually have ruddy faces from drinking blood; they do not avoid daylight.

8. The Writer Robert Browning created a character named porphyria in a poem about a madman who strangles his lover.

9. Modern patients with this rare hereditary disease may suffer for years before their Doctors diagnose the problem correctly, and many of them wish that the illness did not have so many associations with strange stories from Literature and History.

10. The american porphyria foundation is dedicated to increasing public awareness about the disease.

41-2: Capitalizing

Edit the following sentences by capitalizing as needed.

EXAMPLE

T   V
~~t~~he ~~v~~ikings were famous for their sailing ability.

1. ancient icelandic sagas describe viking voyages to lands west of green-land.

2. the sagas mention a norse settlement in a land that might be north america.

3. an american chemist named eben norton horsford believed that the vikings had come to the boston area.

4. he claimed to have found evidence of viking buildings in the nearby towns of cambridge and watertown.

5. around 1860, horsford invented a new kind of baking powder and made a fortune.

6. he used some of his money to commission a statue of leif erikson, which still stands on commonwealth avenue in boston.

7. the professor also believed that a mythical ancient city of gold called norumbega lay along the charles river.

8. a sixteenth-century map made by girolamo verrazano places this lost city in maine, but probably, like el dorado, it never existed.

9. horsford believed that erikson had found the lost city at the mouth of stony brook near waltham, massachusetts, so the professor built a tower to mark the spot.

10. historians have never given much credit to professor horsford's archaeo-logical ideas.

Answers to 22-1

1. subject   2. verb   3. preposition   4. adjective   5. adverb   6. conjunction   7. verb
8. adverb   9. subject   10. pronoun

Answers to 22-2

1. helping verb   2. independent clause   3. independent clause   4. helping verb   5. dependent clause   6. prepositional phrase   7. action verb   8. dependent clause   9. helping verb   10. helping verb

Answers to 23-1
POSSIBLE REVISIONS

1. Such people may also enjoy living in different places. Going from one part of the country to another delights them. They can adapt.
2. Moving frequently is not easy for everyone. Some people like familiar places and situations.
3. Even close relatives may disagree about whether to move from place to place or stay in one town. For example, my sister and I disagree.
4. I have always lived in the same neighborhood. My apartment is near my parents' house, which makes me feel safe and comfortable.
5. I like living near the house where I grew up. I still have many old friends in the area.
6. My sister, on the other hand, has lived in four apartments in the last ten years. One was in California, one was in Chicago, and two were in the Boston area.
7. Her work allows flexibility. In addition, she enjoys traveling and meeting new people. For her, moving is an adventure.
8. I find it difficult to make new friends. Moving to a strange town would be torture for me.
9. I also hate packing. Boxing up all my belongings would take a long time since I am a pack rat.
10. My sister and I have very different views about the ideal way to live. Fortunately, we do not have to choose the same kind of life.

Answers to 23-2
POSSIBLE REVISIONS

1. Summer comes to the Southern Hemisphere in December, making the weather warmest there in February and March.
2. Between late January and early March of 2002, Antarctica was experiencing the warmest summer ever recorded on the icy continent.
3. To see whether the world is really getting warmer, scientists study the ice around the Antarctic continent carefully.
4. In the Antarctic summer of 2002, scientists were watching an ice shelf known as Larsen B, which is on the eastern coast of Antarctica.
5. In most places, the Larsen B ice shelf was about 220 meters thick. But it was melting in the unusually warm temperatures that summer.
6. Between January 31 and March 5, 2002, the Larsen B shelf lost chunks of ice totaling more than 3,200 square kilometers, a mass the size of Rhode Island.
7. Scientists around the world were stunned at the speed of the shelf's breakup.
8. Although climate researchers do not know the exact age of the Larsen B shelf, it has probably existed for at least two thousand years.
9. The average annual temperature in the area around the Larsen B ice shelf has increased by several degrees since the late 1940s.
10. Scientists disagree about the reason for the shelf's disintegration. Some say that the melting ice on top of the shelf caused the breakup, and others blame cracks from the bottom of the shelf.

Answers to 24-1
POSSIBLE REVISIONS

1. A survey once asked people to identify their greatest fear, and the number-one answer was "public speaking."
2. C
3. Many college students have to speak in front of their classmates; in fact, many schools require a public-speaking class.
4. Even experienced public speakers are often nervous before a speech, but being nervous is not necessarily bad.
5. A feeling of nervousness can make a speaker perform well. It means that the person cares about doing a good job.
6. C
7. A speech teacher or a professional speaker can offer some hints. One suggestion is for the speaker to imagine the audience in their underwear.

8. C
9. When a speaker gets up in front of a crowd, he or she may not be able to imagine a funny sight.
10. Planning for nervousness before giving a speech is good common sense; it allows speakers to figure out a way to solve the problem while they are thinking calmly.

Answers to 24-2
POSSIBLE REVISIONS

1. More and more women in the United States are achieving career success, but women with high salaries are less likely than other women to have children.
2. While half of American women who earn over one hundred thousand dollars a year are childless, men who earn high salaries are no less likely than other men to have children.
3. In the business world, both male and female workers put in long hours to get ahead. Then they find it difficult to make time to raise a family.
4. Many male executives are married to women who raise their young children, but female executives are less likely to have a partner who is willing to stay at home.
5. Of course, some women decide not to have any children; many female executives say, however, that they simply ran out of time.
6. Some businesswomen advise younger women to plan ahead. Women, they say, must make arrangements in advance if they want children.
7. Some younger career women believe that they will not have the same problems as previous generations because women today often become successful at an earlier age.
8. A thirty-year-old woman with a good career may feel that she can take some time off. Twenty years ago, few career women of childbearing age were comfortable with such a decision.
9. Young people today are frequently unconcerned about which partner earns more; they also tend to be flexible about which parent stays home with the children.
10. Some powerful American women today regret being childless, but perhaps in the future most career women who want children will have them.

Answers to 25-1

1. subject: person; verb: Does
2. subject: we; verb: are
3. subject: someone; verb: experiences
4. subject: Everyone; verb: does
5. compound subject: pounding heart and a feeling of fear; verb: happen
6. subject: pounding; verb: does
7. subject: emotions; verb: are
8. subject: people; verb: do
9. subject: psychologists; verb: believe
10. compound subject: an emotion and a physical reaction; verb: are

Answers to 25-2

1. is   2. have   3. point   4. are   5. makes
6. is   7. have   8. is   9. are   10. are

Answers to 26-1

1. lost   2. had driven   3. hurt   4. was
5. has had   6. wants   7. had found   8. told
9. turned   10. goes

Answers to 26-2

1. brought   2. introduced   3. have gained
4. have continued   5. see   6. had worn
7. have earned   8. have become   9. called
10. put

Answers to 27-1
POSSIBLE REVISIONS

1. Anyone using a computer to go online has seen Web sites that contain advertising.
2. C
3. However, many people do not realize that some online information that seems reliable comes from advertisers.
4. When my sister used a certain search engine, it gave her results from sites that paid to be mentioned.
5. She and I had not known that advertisers could influence a search engine.
6. C
7. An organization called Consumers Union announced its intention to help Internet users get accurate information.
8. My sister and her boyfriend got their information about evaluating a Web site's trustworthiness from the Consumers Union.
9. The Consumers Union site said that a Web site should identify who created it and where it is produced.
10. C

Answers to 27-2
POSSIBLE REVISIONS

1. However, males and females vent <u>their</u> anger in different ways.
2. My brother and <u>I</u> had very different experiences in high school, but we both had some trouble with other teenagers.
3. My brother was much more likely than <u>I</u> to get into a physical fight with another teenager.
4. According to recent research, girls tend to disguise their aggression.
5. A girl <u>who</u> gets angry with another girl is not likely to have a physical fight with her.
6. Instead, a girl will probably try to hurt another girl psychologically; this happened to my friends and <u>me</u> in high school.
7. Everyone in my group of friends had <u>her</u> turn at being an outsider.
8. When I was an outsider, my friends insulted my clothes and hair or revealed secrets <u>I</u> had told them.
9. My brother and his best friend had <u>their</u> arguments, but they never resorted to the kind of treachery and insults that my friends and I inflicted on one another.
10. No one is certain why girls behave this way, but <u>people</u> who had their female friends turn on them in high school remember how painful the experience was.

Answers to 28-1

1. safely   2. well   3. sleepy   4. dangerous
5. likelier   6. best 7. suddenly   8. more slowly
9. worse   10. most effective

Answers to 28-2

1. Advertisers think that targeting people in their teens and twenties will make products sell <u>well</u>.
2. C
3. Because many businesses are <u>hopeful</u> that showing commercials during television shows with young adult viewers will improve sales, advertising time on those shows is among the <u>most expensive</u> on television.
4. C
5. Instead of being canceled <u>quickly</u>, such a show can make a profit by attracting advertisers who pay better-than-average rates for the commercial time on the show.
6. Advertisers are <u>certain</u> that it is <u>easier</u> to influence a young audience than a middle-aged one.

7. Advertisers believe that older audiences are <u>more loyal</u> to products than younger ones are, so businesses see an older person as a <u>worse</u> customer for a new product.
8. Are <u>more youthful</u> audiences more likely than older ones to be <u>really</u> interested in trying new brands?
9. According to research, a <u>typical</u> middle-aged customer tries new brands more willingly than a teenager tries them, so paying extra money to reach young customers is probably a <u>bad</u> idea.
10. C

Answers to 29-1

1. M   2. D   3. C   4. D   5. C   6. M   7. M
8. C   9. M   10. D

Answers to 29-2
POSSIBLE REVISIONS

1. Nearly every student struggles to write a convincing admissions essay.
2. A student who is a strong writer might even seek help with his or her essay.
3. At some schools, admissions officers, wondering if the essays are actually written by applicants, have begun to ask students to describe the writing help they received.
4. At one prominent university, the essay form that all students must complete says that "all good writers seek feedback, advice, or editing."
5. A few students who are very confident of their writing skills write their essays without help.
6. If those students truthfully report that they did not get any assistance, will admissions committees think that they are lying?
7. Of course, seeking input before submitting written work is always a good idea.
8. Not wanting to give the wrong impression, writers may consult anyone from a friend to a professional for help with an important piece of writing.
9. Admissions officers say that they need to know how much of the admissions essay is a student's own work.
10. While schools may be trying to make the admissions process fair to students who play by the rules, students continue to feel that they are under tremendous pressure when they apply to colleges.

Answers to 30-1
POSSIBLE REVISIONS

1. Wolves were once part of the landscape in many western states, but they were killed off in the twentieth century.
2. When wild wolves from Canada were released in Montana and Wyoming in the mid-1990s, many people were pleased to have wolves back in the western United States.
3. Many ranchers objected to the return of the wolves because they feared for the safety of their livestock.
4. The wolves were endangered; therefore, hunting them was illegal.
5. When unhappy ranchers opposed the wolves' presence, the government promised to kill any wolf that harmed livestock.
6. Ranchers demanded compensation for animals killed by wolves; then, environmental groups agreed to pay for livestock losses.
7. Wolf policies became controversial in 2002 after the government paid for the killing of an entire wolf pack.
8. The government spent fifteen thousand dollars to hunt down the pack even though the wolves killed just a few hundred dollars worth of livestock.
9. The wolves were wearing radio collars, and government hunters were able to track the wolves with the help of those collars.
10. A wildlife organization had donated the collars to help biologists; the group decided not to provide any more radio collars.

Answers to 30-2
POSSIBLE REVISIONS

1. These meteors are visible on a clear night, and they have been admired by stargazers for thousands of years.
2. Sometimes they burn up completely in space, but at other times, they fall to earth.
3. Ancient Romans worshiped the meteorites that landed on earth because they considered them "stones from heaven."
4. Later observers were more skeptical; in fact, scientists in the eighteenth century did not believe meteorites existed.
5. After a meteor shower happened in broad daylight in France in 1803, most people began to believe in the reality of meteorites.
6. Meteorites tend to land most often in just a few places; in the United States, the most

meteorites are in Texas, Kansas, New Mexico, and Colorado.
7. While Australia and Antarctica are rich in meteorites, the Sahara Desert may be the best place on earth for locating them.
8. Meteorites contain a great deal of iron, so some people use magnets to find them.
9. Meteorites are often darkly colored or strangely marked, and collectors pay high prices for them.
10. When one collector recently sold a rare specimen, he received $2 million for it.

Answers to 31-1
POSSIBLE REVISIONS

1. In the United States, immigrants in many areas not only have neighbors from their native country but also shop at markets with familiar foods.
2. In the past, many immigrants found that small ethnic markets served their needs better than large supermarkets.
3. Supermarkets are now trying to attract shoppers by selling ethnic produce, mainly from Asian, Central American, and South American countries.
4. For many shoppers, finding everything in one store is better than getting a few items in one place and the rest in another.
5. C
6. C
7. On the other hand, if a customer can buy both ethnic food and milk, eggs, and shampoo at the same supermarket, the supermarket may win a loyal shopper.
8. Supermarkets lose money and business by stocking items that people do not want or by failing to stock items that customers demand.
9. C
10. Ethnic food, such as dishes from India and Thailand, are also becoming increasingly popular among nonimmigrant Americans.

Answers to 31-2
POSSIBLE REVISIONS

1. Chores such as doing the laundry, cleaning the house, and washing the dishes take time even when people use modern appliances to help.
2. Many people feel that household jobs are not only boring but also time-consuming.
3. Twenty years ago, many people believed

that men and women would soon share household chores equally, spend the same amount of time with their children, and both work outside the home.

4. However, most working husbands today neither do half of the housework nor spend as much time with their children as most working wives do.

5. Wives in 1965 most often stayed at home and raised children full-time.

6. Today, when a majority of young and middle-aged wives work outside the home, women, on average, spend twice as much time doing housework as men spend.

7. Many people, both men and women, view housework as less important than an office job.

8. Although Americans say that children are very important, many people respect a person who works outside the home more than a person who stays home to care for children.

9. Will the next generation of young men do more housework and help raise the children?

10. If today's boys are to grow up to do their fair share of work at home, their parents must teach them the importance of that work, make them see that housework is the responsibility of both husbands and wives, and set a good example.

Answers to 32-1
POSSIBLE REVISIONS

1. Obesity, an increasing problem in the United States, affects one out of eight American schoolchildren.

2. Researchers see many reasons for widespread obesity, blaming factors such as fast food, parents, schools, and advertisements.

3. Fast-food restaurants, a major source of fat in the American diet, offer larger portions now than in previous decades.

4. French fries at McDonald's are one example, now appearing in a "super size" that is three times as large as the portion sold in 1955.

5. Surrounded with junk food and soft drinks instead of healthy snacks, children also pick up bad eating habits at home.

6. Many parents who mean well teach their children to prize candy and desserts by using them as rewards or special treats.

7. Schools are not teaching good nutrition

either, often allowing snack and soft drink companies to advertise or sell products inside the school.

8. Bombarded with food advertising at home and at school, schoolchildren often give in to advertisements even if they do not want or need the food.

9. Physical activity, which is an important way to fight obesity, is no longer a significant part of everyday life for many children.

10. Obesity, a major cause of premature death in this country, will become a larger problem if today's overweight children become overweight adults.

Answers to 32-2
POSSIBLE REVISIONS

1. Email, her greatest delight, allows her to keep in touch with her grandchildren.

2. Her hearing, which is getting worse with time, prevents her from understanding some spoken words.

3. Frustrated by many telephone conversations these days, my grandmother loves having another way to contact friends and family quickly.

4. She has stopped listening to television and radio newscasters, who don't provide information that is useful to her.

5. My grandmother, a diabetic, finds out about the latest treatments and research online.

6. Fascinated with opera, she has found dozens of Web sites about her favorite singers and composers.

7. Americans over age sixty-five, the fastest-growing segment of the population, have not generally been quick to adapt to the computer age.

8. Wanting to communicate with loved ones and find information, older women are taking up computing faster than any other group of people in the United States.

9. Remaining young at heart, my grandmother sees the Internet as a way of keeping in touch with the most enjoyable parts of her life.

10. However, she hasn't yet adapted to cellular phones, another product of the technology age.

Answers to 33-1

1. For many years, Americans have not worried much about pollution in other countries.

2. C

3. Enormous dust storms in China have been causing high levels of smog on the American West Coast.
4. Chinese farmers keep using many dangerous chemicals that are not allowed in the United States.
5. Dust storms can pick up these chemicals in China and carry them across the Pacific Ocean.
6. C
7. C
8. A scientist who is investigating African dust in the United States has found viruses in the dust.
9. Did viruses migrate from Africa to the United States on particles of dust?
10. It seems that Americans will soon have to care about pollution problems around the world.

Answers to 33-2

1. People in many parts of the world expect to pay much higher prices for gasoline than Americans do.
2. In the United States, low gasoline prices surprise visitors from Europe and Asia.
3. However, most Americans with cars know how expensive owning a car can be.
4. In much of this country, people spend almost as much money on transportation as they spend on housing.
5. For most people, filling up the gas tank is usually only a small part of the cost of car ownership.
6. A person who buys a car may not be aware of the other expenses involved, such as insurance, car payments, and repairs.
7. Because the cost of living in many cities is so high, people in much of the country live in homes many miles from their jobs.
8. They live in areas that do not have public transportation.
9. Suburban housing does not cost as much as living in town, but the cost of owning a car can make the suburbs more expensive.
10. A person thinking of moving far from town to a place where housing is inexpensive should get some advice about the cost of transportation.

Answers to 34-1
POSSIBLE REVISIONS

1. Many Americans eat snack foods loaded with fat, calories, and salt almost every day.

2. According to a recent study of the American diet, almost half of the home-cooked meals served in this country contain no vegetables.
3. The study of the American diet may not have counted potato chips as a vegetable.
4. Americans consume more potato chips than any other snack food, over a billion pounds a year.
5. Although the potato was originally South American, the potato chip was invented by a chef in Saratoga Springs, New York.
6. Other foods invented in the United States include the ice cream cone and the hamburger.
7. Surprisingly, fortune cookies and chop suey, common in many Chinese restaurants, were also created in the United States.
8. The Popsicle and the Twinkie, beloved by American children now and in the past, were also invented in this country.
9. Another American innovation was the prepared mix; the first one sold was for pancakes.
10. With the enormous international success of fast food, another American invention, should Americans be proud of their contribution to world cuisine?

Answers to 34-2
POSSIBLE REVISIONS

1. Americans have less vacation time than people in any other industrialized country have.
2. On average, the head of an American company gives the workers just thirteen days out of each year as vacation time.
3. Thirteen days is a very short time compared to the average number of vacation days in Italy.
4. Italian workers receive an average of forty-two days of vacation time per year.
5. Europeans in general get a huge amount of vacation time, with French and German workers averaging thirty-six days a year and British workers getting twenty-eight.
6. Most Americans will never get a month off from work every year.
7. Even in Japan, where employees are noted for working long hours, the average vacation time is twenty-five days per year.
8. The saddest thing about all of this is that many Americans don't even take the vacations they have earned.

9. One out of six U.S. workers fails to use annual vacation time because he or she feels obliged to work instead.
10. Doctors say that vacations help workers eliminate job stress.

Answers to 35-1

1. losing   2. mind   3. supposed   4. sit
5. they're   6. It's   7. except   8. have
9. conscious   10. advice

Answers to 35-2

1. to   2. passed   3. by; effect   4. were; knew
5. raps; its   6. whose   7. holes   8. heard
9. find   10. quiet

Answers to 36-1

1. Traditional   2. cities; sharing   3. participate
4. reckless; several   5. receive   6. activate
7. usually; necessary   8. occasion   9. recognize;
commitment   10. excellent; probably

Answers to 36-2

1. occasional   2. arguments   3. believe
4. develop   5. privileges   6. annoying
7. professional   8. chronically   9. immediately
10. truly

Answers to 37-1

1. Any treatment that promises to make people look younger is almost guaranteed to attract customers, so researchers keep developing antiaging formulas.
2. Even though most treatments are expensive, they are becoming increasingly popular among men as well as women.
3. A drug called botulinum toxin, a form of a paralyzing poison, was approved for medical use by the Food and Drug Administration.
4. For patients with severe muscle contractions, botulinum toxin was a proven treatment.
5. The word quickly spread that botulinum toxin, known as "Botox," also effectively removed facial wrinkles and lines.
6. Botox was not approved for cosmetic uses, yet many healthy people began asking doctors to inject them with it.
7. C
8. However, after too much Botox, parts of a person's face may appear strangely unable to move.
9. Side effects of Botox treatments can include headaches, nausea, and drooping eyelids.
10. In the spring of 2002, Botox was approved for use in cosmetic treatments, a develop-

ment that simply acknowledged how the drug was already being used.

Answers to 37-2

1. Abrams, who was born around 1863, was one of the most successful quacks in medical history.
2. In 1910, Abrams claimed that he could cure diseases by tapping on a patient's spine.
3. The dawn of the electronic age arrived, and Abrams introduced electronic machines to a gullible public.
4. When Americans became fascinated with radio, Abrams announced that he could use radios to diagnose diseases.
5. Abrams's theory of electronic diagnosis, called the Electronic Reactions of Abrams, involved an elaborate machine called a dynamizer.
6. The dynamizer analyzed a sample of blood drawn while a patient faced west.
7. Skeptics supplied sheep blood, chicken blood, and red ink.
8. When the dynamizer diagnosed fatal illnesses, Dr. Abrams informed the skeptics that another machine, the oscilloclast, could cure them for $250.
9. After a thorough investigation of Abrams's techniques, *Scientific American* called the dynamizer "utterly worthless."
10. Abrams, who died on January 13, 1924, fooled enough people to leave behind an estate worth $2 million.

Answers to 38-1

1. She's; 0's; 1's   2. SETI's; scans   3. scientists
4. telescope's; there's   5. don't   6. hundreds
7. theirs; they'd; weren't   8. It's   9. hers
10. she'll; scientists'

Answers to 38-2

1. its; sites   2. bulldozer's   3. computers'; don't
4. dot-coms   5. Analysts'; jobs 6. hours'; parts
7. workers'   8. it's   9. Doesn't; it'd   10. yours;
you're

Answers to 39-1

1. I asked him, "What's it called?"
2. He held up a book that had been mine, *The Collected Stories of Beatrix Potter.*
3. He told me, "It's 'The Tale of Peter Rabbit' by Beatrix Potter."
4. My favorite stories from the collection were "The Tale of Benjamin Bunny," "The Tale

of the Flopsy Bunnies," and "The Tale of Mrs. Tiggy-Winkle."

5. Picking up the book, I told him, "Show me the part of the story you don't understand."

6. "It says that the sparrows 'implored him to exert himself,'" he said.

7. How stupid did I feel when I said, "I need a dictionary to look up one of those words"?

8. My mother overheard us and told him that the sparrows wanted Peter Rabbit to try very hard to escape.

9. "You never seem foolish for looking up a word," she said to us.

10. She said that I would only look foolish if I pretended to know a word that I didn't understand.

Answers to 39-2

1. "I'm overweight, but I'm in excellent health," she said.

2. Aunt Catherine has a nursing degree from the Columbia College of Nursing.

3. After her husband lost his job, she contacted an insurance company and asked how much it would cost to get a family insurance policy.

4. The letter she received said, "We're sorry, but your weight puts you at risk."

5. "My cholesterol level and blood pressure are excellent," she said, "and I exercise regularly."

6. She showed me a newspaper article called, "Is Obesity a Disease or Just a Symptom?"

7. "The author says right here, 'Being overweight is not necessarily life threatening,'" she said.

8. C

9. She got a letter from him that said, "Catherine is fit and will probably live to a ripe old age."

10. Aunt Catherine is still trying to find an insurance company that recognizes that she can be both healthy and overweight.

Answers to 40-1
POSSIBLE REVISIONS

1. Drug addiction often leads to serious medical problems; it is, therefore, considered a disease.

2. Some people (and no one knows which people) are more likely than others to become addicts.

3. Diagnostic tests are not available to identify an addiction-prone person.

4. A tendency toward drug addiction may be genetic; it may also be an accident of brain chemistry.

5. The drugs that cause serious addiction problems may be those substances traditionally considered most dangerous: heroin, crack cocaine, and powdered cocaine.

6. However, marijuana (now a much more potent drug than it was thirty years ago) also causes dependence among some young people.

7. According to a 2001 poll, 40 percent of American eighteen-year-olds have smoked marijuana at least once.

8. Some of these young people will react to super-potent marijuana by showing signs of psychological addiction: needing the drug daily, needing larger and larger amounts of it, spending a lot of money and effort to get it, and lying about drug use to friends and family.

9. Some teenagers who feel that their marijuana use causes problems do quit; however, over two-thirds of them will start smoking it again.

10. Most teenagers do not realize that there can be long-term consequences—including addiction—of trying marijuana.

Answers to 40-2
POSSIBLE REVISIONS

1. Quaggas—native to South Africa—once roamed the plains by the thousands.

2. Boer settlers in the region killed off quaggas for several reasons: The animals competed with livestock for scarce grass, they were a source of food, and their hides were striking.

3. Soon, the extinction of the quagga was complete; the last wild quagga died in 1878, and the last quagga in captivity died in the Amsterdam Zoo in 1883.

4. In the 1980s, an analysis of DNA from a quagga hide showed that quaggas (long considered a unique species) were a subspecies of the Burchell's zebra.

5. The Hottentots of South Africa had always used the term "quagga"—a word imitating the creatures' cry—to name both Burchell's zebra and the extinct quagga.

6. The Quagga Project is a breeding program in South Africa; scientists select Burchell's zebras for quagga-like coloring and markings.

7. The program has had some success since its 1987 beginnings: The zebras in the breeding program have fainter stripes on their backs and rumps, and they are noticeably browner than traditional Burchell's zebras.

8. Quagga Project scientists hope that they may be retrieving genes once found in wild quaggas (there is no way to be certain since no genetic material from extinct quaggas survives).

9. The Quagga Project wants to return animals that look like the long-lost quagga to the South African plains.

10. The project would not exactly bring quaggas back from extinction; however, many people still hope to see the project succeed.

Answers to 41-1

1. An article in a British medical journal once suggested that the king was suffering from porphyria, a rare blood disease.

2. This idea was used in Alan Bennett's play *The Madness of King George* and the movie with the same name.

3. The play and movie suggested that George's porphyria contributed to his anger at the American colonies and, therefore, to the Revolutionary War.

4. Historians have no way of knowing if the monarch's first period of insanity, during which Parliament nearly declared him unfit to rule, was actually caused by porphyria, but it may have been.

5. Porphyria has also been linked by some people to the popular conception of vampires.

6. One form of porphyria causes sufferers' skin to blister when it is exposed to the sun, so, like Dracula in Bram Stoker's novel, they stay indoors during the day.

7. The vampires of folklore in stories from Balkan countries, however, usually have ruddy faces from drinking blood; they do not avoid daylight.

8. The writer Robert Browning created a character named Porphyria in a poem about a madman who strangles his lover.

9. Modern patients with this rare hereditary disease may suffer for years before their doctors diagnose the problem correctly, and many of them wish that the illness did not have so many associations with strange stories from literature and history.

10. The American Porphyria Foundation is dedicated to increasing public awareness about the disease.

Answers to 41-2

1. Ancient Icelandic sagas describe Viking voyages to lands west of Greenland.

2. The sagas mention a Norse settlement in a land that might be North America.

3. An American chemist named Eben Norton Horsford believed that the Vikings had come to the Boston area.

4. He claimed to have found evidence of Viking buildings in the nearby towns of Cambridge and Watertown.

5. Around 1860, Horsford invented a new kind of baking powder and made a fortune.

6. He used some of his money to commission a statue of Leif Erikson, which still stands on Commonwealth Avenue in Boston.

7. The professor also believed that a mythical ancient city of gold called Norumbega lay along the Charles River.

8. A sixteenth-century map made by Girolamo Verrazano places this lost city in Maine, but probably, like El Dorado, it never existed.

9. Horsford believed that Erikson had found the lost city at the mouth of Stony Brook near Waltham, Massachusetts, so the professor built a tower to mark the spot.

10. Historians have never given much credit to Professor Horsford's archaeological ideas.

Quick Review Charts
(*Chapters 22–34*)

Quick Review Chart: Fragments

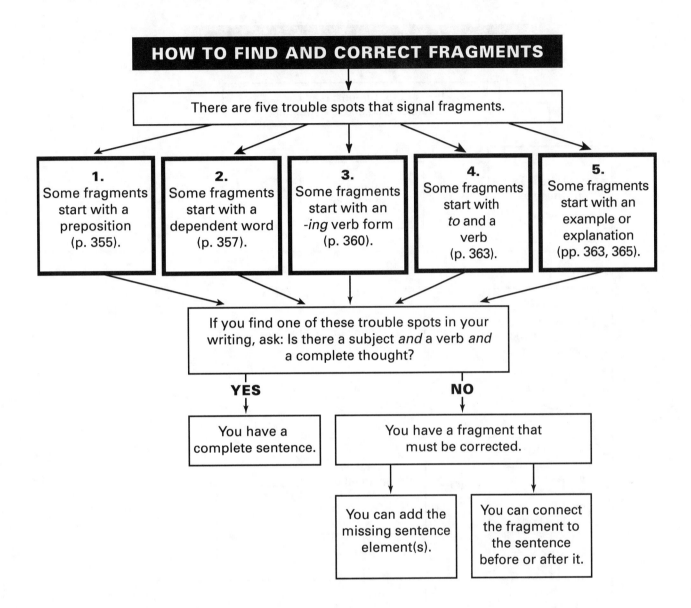

HOW TO FIND AND CORRECT FRAGMENTS

There are five trouble spots that signal fragments.

1.
Some fragments start with a preposition (p. 355).

2.
Some fragments start with a dependent word (p. 357).

3.
Some fragments start with an *-ing* verb form (p. 360).

4.
Some fragments start with *to* and a verb (p. 363).

5.
Some fragments start with an example or explanation (pp. 363, 365).

If you find one of these trouble spots in your writing, ask: Is there a subject *and* a verb *and* a complete thought?

YES

You have a complete sentence.

NO

You have a fragment that must be corrected.

You can add the missing sentence element(s).

You can connect the fragment to the sentence before or after it.

Quick Review Chart: Run-Ons

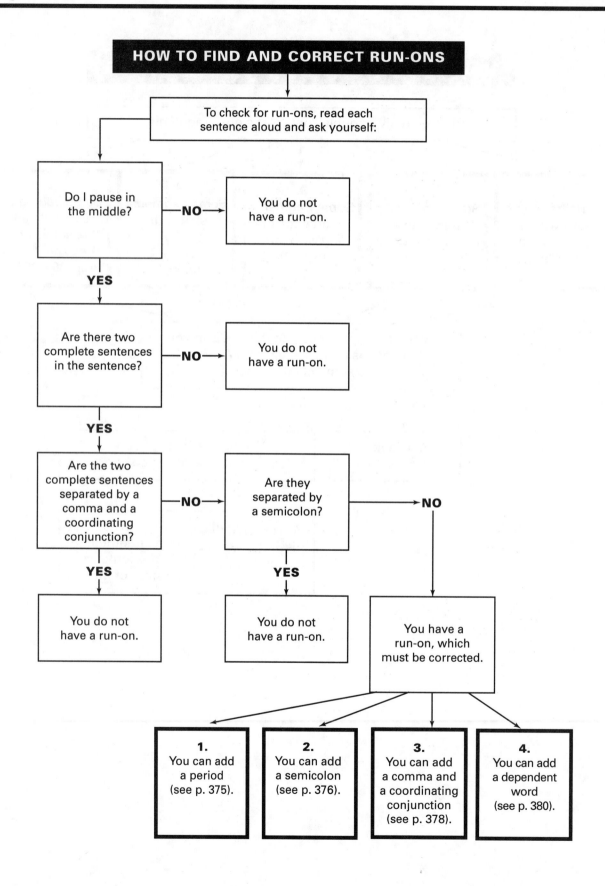

Quick Review Chart: Problems with Subject–Verb Agreement

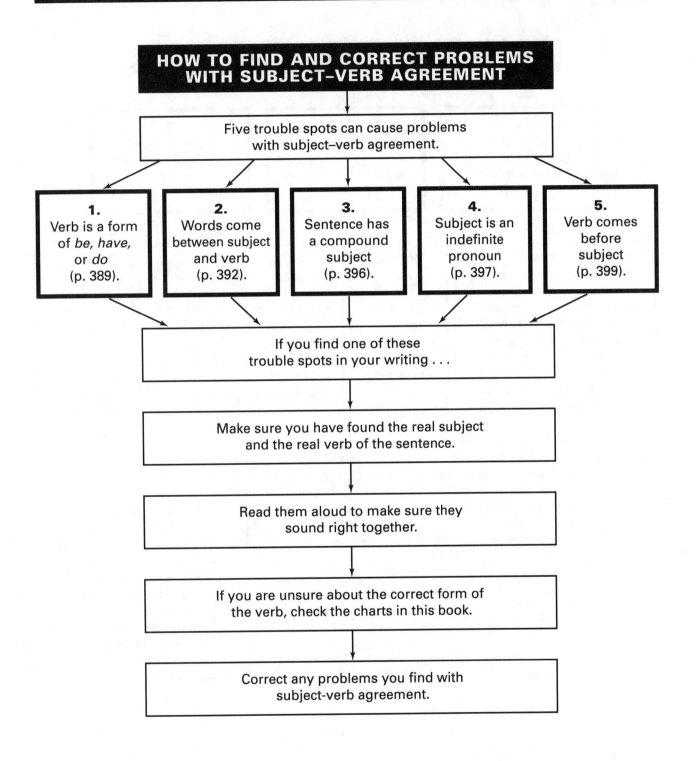

HOW TO FIND AND CORRECT PROBLEMS WITH SUBJECT–VERB AGREEMENT

Five trouble spots can cause problems with subject–verb agreement.

1. Verb is a form of *be, have,* or *do* (p. 389).

2. Words come between subject and verb (p. 392).

3. Sentence has a compound subject (p. 396).

4. Subject is an indefinite pronoun (p. 397).

5. Verb comes before subject (p. 399).

If you find one of these trouble spots in your writing . . .

Make sure you have found the real subject and the real verb of the sentence.

Read them aloud to make sure they sound right together.

If you are unsure about the correct form of the verb, check the charts in this book.

Correct any problems you find with subject-verb agreement.

Quick Review Chart: Verb Problems

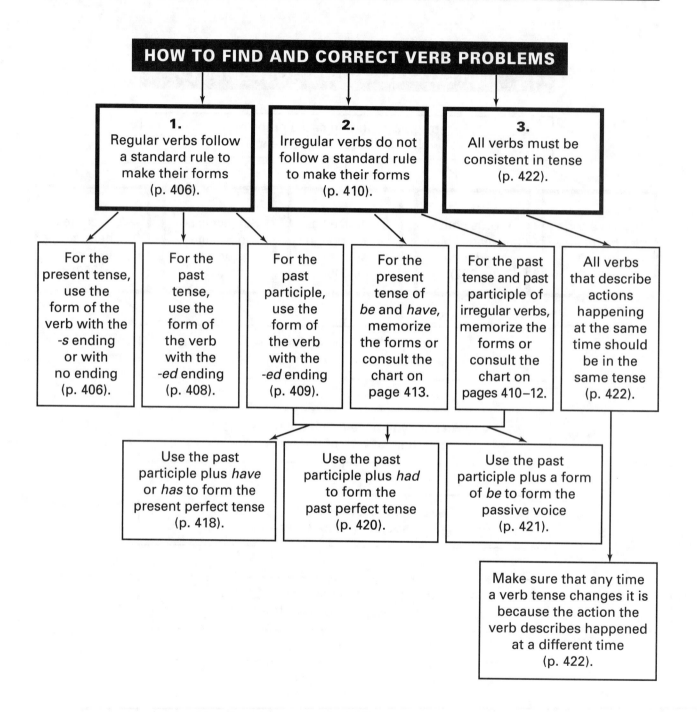

HOW TO FIND AND CORRECT VERB PROBLEMS

1.
Regular verbs follow a standard rule to make their forms (p. 406).

2.
Irregular verbs do not follow a standard rule to make their forms (p. 410).

3.
All verbs must be consistent in tense (p. 422).

For the present tense, use the form of the verb with the -*s* ending or with no ending (p. 406).

For the past tense, use the form of the verb with the -*ed* ending (p. 408).

For the past participle, use the form of the verb with the -*ed* ending (p. 409).

For the present tense of *be* and *have*, memorize the forms or consult the chart on page 413.

For the past tense and past participle of irregular verbs, memorize the forms or consult the chart on pages 410–12.

All verbs that describe actions happening at the same time should be in the same tense (p. 422).

Use the past participle plus *have* or *has* to form the present perfect tense (p. 418).

Use the past participle plus *had* to form the past perfect tense (p. 420).

Use the past participle plus a form of *be* to form the passive voice (p. 421).

Make sure that any time a verb tense changes it is because the action the verb describes happened at a different time (p. 422).

Quick Review Chart: Pronouns

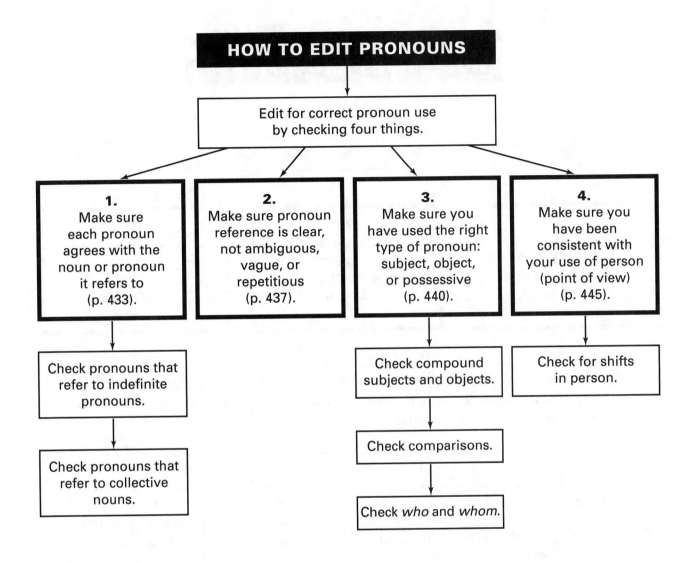

HOW TO EDIT PRONOUNS

Edit for correct pronoun use
by checking four things.

1.
Make sure
each pronoun
agrees with the
noun or pronoun
it refers to
(p. 433).

2.
Make sure pronoun
reference is clear,
not ambiguous,
vague, or
repetitious
(p. 437).

3.
Make sure you
have used the right
type of pronoun:
subject, object,
or possessive
(p. 440).

4.
Make sure you
have been
consistent with
your use of person
(point of view)
(p. 445).

Check pronouns that
refer to indefinite
pronouns.

Check pronouns that
refer to collective
nouns.

Check compound
subjects and objects.

Check for shifts
in person.

Check comparisons.

Check *who* and *whom.*

Quick Review Chart: Adjectives and Adverbs

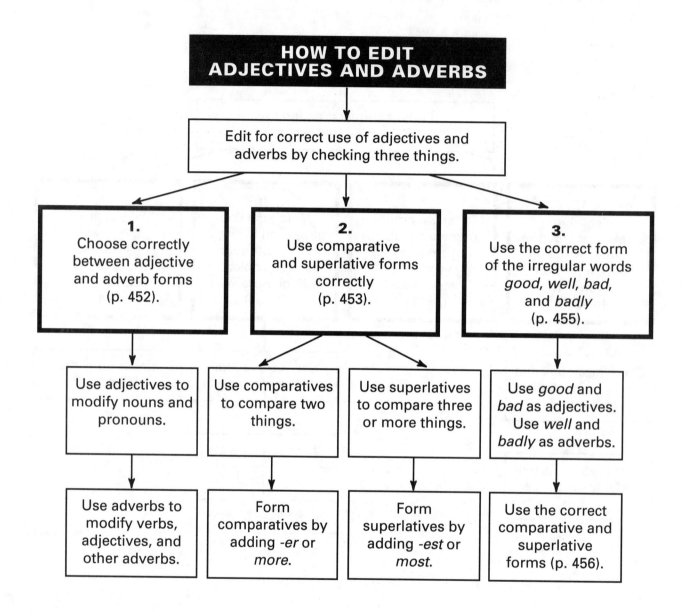

HOW TO EDIT ADJECTIVES AND ADVERBS

Edit for correct use of adjectives and adverbs by checking three things.

1.
Choose correctly between adjective and adverb forms (p. 452).

2.
Use comparative and superlative forms correctly (p. 453).

3.
Use the correct form of the irregular words *good, well, bad,* and *badly* (p. 455).

Use adjectives to modify nouns and pronouns.

Use comparatives to compare two things.

Use superlatives to compare three or more things.

Use *good* and *bad* as adjectives. Use *well* and *badly* as adverbs.

Use adverbs to modify verbs, adjectives, and other adverbs.

Form comparatives by adding *-er* or *more.*

Form superlatives by adding *-est* or *most.*

Use the correct comparative and superlative forms (p. 456).

Quick Review Chart: Misplaced and Dangling Modifiers

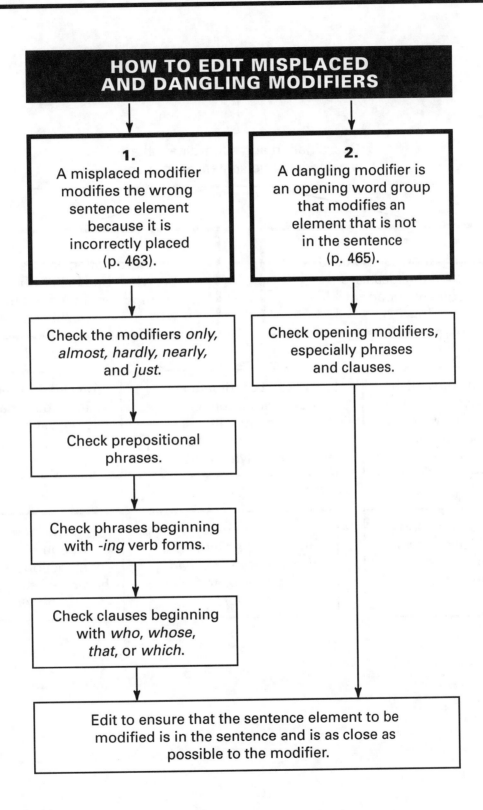

HOW TO EDIT MISPLACED AND DANGLING MODIFIERS

1.
A misplaced modifier modifies the wrong sentence element because it is incorrectly placed (p. 463).

2.
A dangling modifier is an opening word group that modifies an element that is not in the sentence (p. 465).

Check the modifiers *only, almost, hardly, nearly,* and *just*.

Check opening modifiers, especially phrases and clauses.

Check prepositional phrases.

Check phrases beginning with *-ing* verb forms.

Check clauses beginning with *who, whose, that,* or *which*.

Edit to ensure that the sentence element to be modified is in the sentence and is as close as possible to the modifier.

Quick Review Chart: Coordination and Subordination

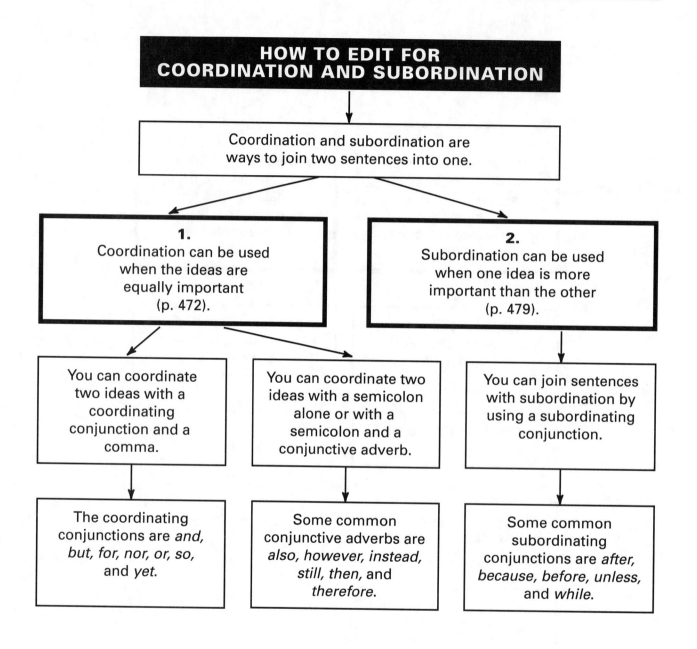

HOW TO EDIT FOR COORDINATION AND SUBORDINATION

Coordination and subordination are ways to join two sentences into one.

1.
Coordination can be used when the ideas are equally important (p. 472).

2.
Subordination can be used when one idea is more important than the other (p. 479).

You can coordinate two ideas with a coordinating conjunction and a comma.

You can coordinate two ideas with a semicolon alone or with a semicolon and a conjunctive adverb.

You can join sentences with subordination by using a subordinating conjunction.

The coordinating conjunctions are *and, but, for, nor, or, so,* and *yet*.

Some common conjunctive adverbs are *also, however, instead, still, then,* and *therefore*.

Some common subordinating conjunctions are *after, because, before, unless,* and *while*.

Quick Review Chart: Parallelism

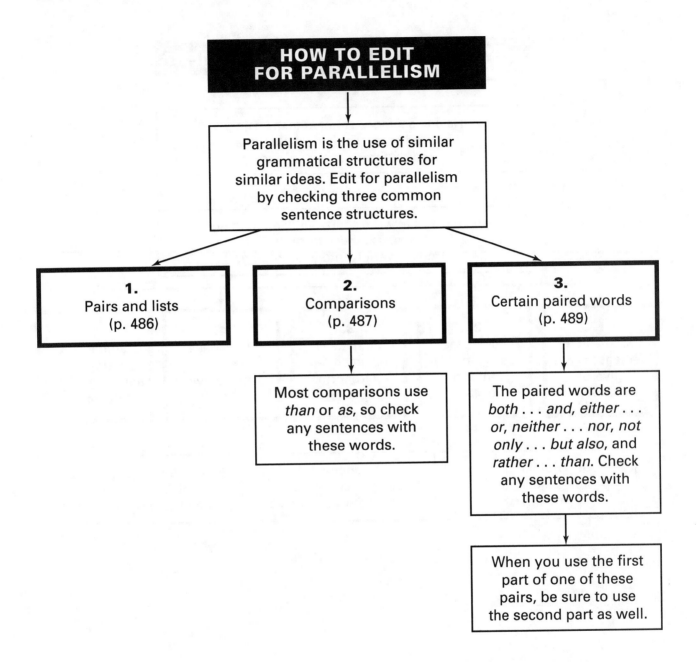

HOW TO EDIT FOR PARALLELISM

Parallelism is the use of similar grammatical structures for similar ideas. Edit for parallelism by checking three common sentence structures.

1.
Pairs and lists
(p. 486)

2.
Comparisons
(p. 487)

3.
Certain paired words
(p. 489)

Most comparisons use *than* or *as*, so check any sentences with these words.

The paired words are *both . . . and, either . . . or, neither . . . nor, not only . . . but also*, and *rather . . . than*. Check any sentences with these words.

When you use the first part of one of these pairs, be sure to use the second part as well.

Quick Review Chart: Sentence Variety

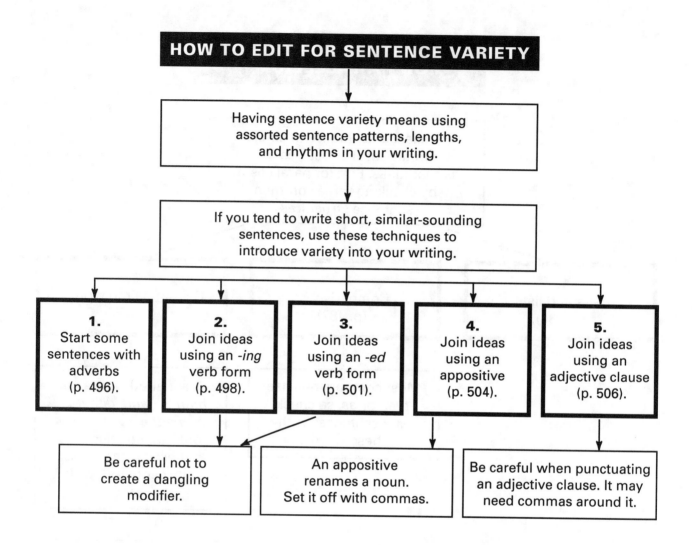

HOW TO EDIT FOR SENTENCE VARIETY

Having sentence variety means using assorted sentence patterns, lengths, and rhythms in your writing.

If you tend to write short, similar-sounding sentences, use these techniques to introduce variety into your writing.

1. Start some sentences with adverbs (p. 496).

2. Join ideas using an *-ing* verb form (p. 498).

3. Join ideas using an *-ed* verb form (p. 501).

4. Join ideas using an appositive (p. 504).

5. Join ideas using an adjective clause (p. 506).

Be careful not to create a dangling modifier.

An appositive renames a noun. Set it off with commas.

Be careful when punctuating an adjective clause. It may need commas around it.

Quick Review Chart: Word Choice

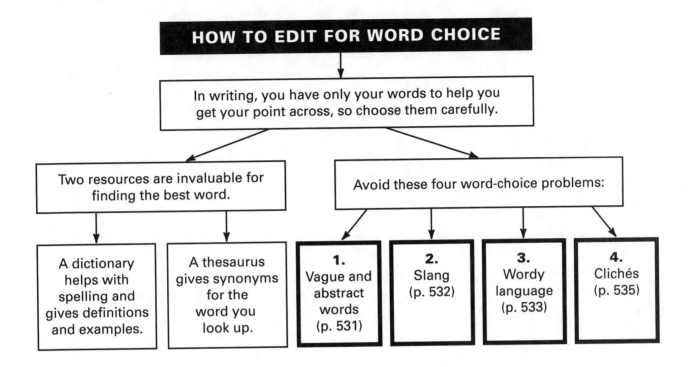

HOW TO EDIT FOR WORD CHOICE

In writing, you have only your words to help you get your point across, so choose them carefully.

Two resources are invaluable for finding the best word.

Avoid these four word-choice problems:

A dictionary helps with spelling and gives definitions and examples.

A thesaurus gives synonyms for the word you look up.

1. Vague and abstract words (p. 531)

2. Slang (p. 532)

3. Wordy language (p. 533)

4. Clichés (p. 535)